Jump-Start
^{That} Job Search

✔ **Get on Task**

✔ **Stay on Task**

✔ **Land That Job**

By Linda L. King, PCC
Certified Life Coach, ADHD Coach

Thanks to Alain Riazuelo, IAP/UPMC/CNRS, for use of black hole image on page 23

Acknowledgments

I could never have written this book without the help of the wonderful staff of the North Shore Career Center (NSCC) in Salem, MA. I've given many presentations to their professional networking groups and when I called Executive Director Mark Whitmore to ask if a book like this would be a useful tool for job seekers, his response was an enthusiastic "Yes!" Mark's support, encouragement, and feedback have been instrumental in developing and completing this workbook.

Two of Mark's staff members, Deborah Barnes and Wolfgang Koch, have spent much time working with me to make sure this book really does serve the needs of job seekers—both the newly-seeking and the long-term unemployed. Deborah and Wolfgang both read my first draft and gave invaluable suggestions for making it more robust and useful. What I didn't know at the time was that they both were experienced editors and applied their expertise as they read—something I had no idea they would do. Deborah also contributed her wisdom about the importance of attitude on page 107.

It was important to present all of this information to actual job seekers before it was published. The folks at NSCC opened their doors, allowing me to run prototype workshops for their clients. I could not have executed these workshops without Wolfgang's wonderful support. He did everything needed to make the necessary preparations at NSCC, from promoting the workshops to ensuring thorough completion of even the most mundane support tasks. I could not be more appreciative of Wolfgang's many efforts and skills, not the least of which are his prompt and cheerful communications. Thanks to him, our workshops proceeded like clockwork and the response from the participants was gratifyingly enthusiastic.

Thanks to Theresa Lavender and Chris Shank at OhioMeansJobs-Meigs County, a One-Stop career center in southern Ohio. It was good to learn about a One-Stop in a different demographic and geographic location, and they were very gracious in sharing their time and giving me lots of good information.

Much appreciation to Gail Griffin at the Vocational Rehabilitation Center (VRC) in Malden, MA for going over my chapter on VRCs and making sure that my information was correct. Many thanks to Joyce and David Adamson for their excellent proofreading.

I'm always grateful to my editor, Annie Duvall, who is a delight to work with and does a great job tightening up or reworking my language when needed. She finds all those little errors that could so easily slip through the cracks without her eagle-eye. When I get stuck, I know I can write whatever I'm trying to say and she will work her magic to clean it up.

Keri Adams-Gagne has worked with me from the very beginning of my coaching business, designing my brochures, business cards, and the covers of my first book. Keri always asks me for my thoughts and then turns them into something beautiful. She not only designed the covers of this book, but did the inside design as well.

A shout-out to my dear brother, Richard King, who is so proud of his little sister and is there for me when I need him. I truly appreciate having Rich's faith and support. Much appreciation to my dear friend Martha Moore, who provided accountability for me when I was flagging a bit. Making commitments to her about what I planned to accomplish daily and weekly kept me on track.

And finally, many thanks to my technical adviser, preliminary editor, and beloved husband Walt Tuvell. He always rescues me when I fight with technology. He read the first draft of this book and suggested many good changes. Walt has enthusiastically supported of all of my efforts to develop this book and its corresponding workshop.

Table of Contents

Part Three: Creating a Master Plan and Schedule

Part Four: Strategies for Planning Your Week

Part Five: Wrapping It Up

Introduction

Job hunting can be an emotional roller coaster. The emotions involved—hope, optimism, depression, despair—can sometimes all be experienced in a the span of a day, or even an hour. I know. I've been there. Some years ago, my husband, the main breadwinner at the time, lost his job. It was right after the financial crash of 2008, plus he was a "mature worker." Even though I wasn't the one looking for the job, I went through the process with him and I know there were times when it was brutal.

Avoidance was very enticing. But even though there were days that I'm sure he wanted to pull the covers over his head, he was constantly and proactively out there looking for new leads and new openings, and submitting applications. So often, those applications disappeared into the abyss, never to be heard from again. There were many times when what appeared to be a very promising lead fell through. It was hardly comforting to be told, "You were our second choice. Please keep in touch." But he persevered. The job market slowly recovered and he ended up finding a very good job.

If you are in the process of a job search, either because you've just entered the job market or because you've become unemployed, you may already know what you *should* be doing. But sometimes doing what you "know" is hard. In this book you will find tools to get you started, help you overcome procrastination, and set and reach realistic goals.

Admittedly, there are some people who hit the ground running when they start their search. They are proactive, motivated, and inspired. Whether because of fear or optimism, they are "on the case," using their time well, spending the better part of every day working on finding employment. But they are the exception rather than the rule, and they are probably not reading this book. If you're on the other end of the spectrum you have plenty of company.

Like most job searchers, you will probably experience rejection in the process. You'll fill out online applications that won't ever be acknowledged. If you did not leave your previous job by choice, you might feel depressed or defeated, even if your unemployment has nothing to do with your performance or ability. You might feel anxious—how long will it take to find another job? What will I do for money? Will I have to get more training? What if I can't find another job?

Add to that the fact that there are no longer deadlines, no structure, and no accountability to anyone but yourself. Being unemployed can "do a number" on your stress level and fears. I'm not trying to paint a doom-and-gloom picture here. I'm saying that the feelings you may be experiencing are perfectly *normal*, and that although the journey can be tough, the best way to see your worst fears come true is to avoid the search altogether.

If you resonate with the above, please be reassured. Losing a job is a life change, similar in intensity to losing a spouse through death or going through a divorce. But it is survivable. Similarly, finding the right job is like finding the right mate and having a good match is paramount to happiness and life satisfaction. To find that right job you have to be proactive and you have to get out there.

It is not hopeless, and *there is a way to go from pessimistic to productive.* I've worked with job seekers who have been sidetracked for over six months and gotten them back on track. I regularly give talks to employment and networking groups, and get asked back multiple times. Why? Because the advice that I give to my clients, and in my presentations, is both effective and simple to implement.

You'll start out by looking at your priorities and then creating a job-search action plan. You'll learn simple and highly-effective strategies and approaches to get going and keep going. The tools in this book are especially helpful for those tasks you are avoiding.

You *can* get going, and keep going, on your search for employment. There are no complicated systems in this book—just simple, easy-to-implement tools that can help you stop procrastinating and get moving. Despite what may look like evidence to the contrary, you *can* create structure and accountability in a situation where it seems like there are neither. And once you find employment, you can use these same techniques for effective time management on the job and in your personal life as well. They work for me in my own life, they work for my clients, and they can work for you too.

As the ancient Chinese philosopher Lao-Tzu said, "A journey of a thousand miles begins with a single step." By picking up this book, you have already taken that first step. And every page you read, every exercise you work on, every question you answer, is one more step. You can do it. You can stay focused and productive. And you *can* find that job! Let's start the journey together.

Part One:

Getting Started

How to Use This Book

Congratulations! By buying this book, and then actually opening it, you have already taken the first two steps in the right direction towards finding a job. This book will help you create both a detailed job-search action plan and a schedule to carry it out. You will gain tools and strategies to use every day on your job search. Your time will be spent more productively, and you can feel good about your efforts at the end of the day.

If you are not using this book as a participant in a workshop, here are some suggestions on how you can most effectively use this book as your own private job-search workshop:

Plan Your Approach

- Plan on working on the book at least 2–3 times per week.
- Decide to spend 1–2 hours per session reading the text and working through the exercises.
- Know when your daily energy is at a peak and schedule your sessions for that time of day.
- Schedule your sessions on your calendar just as you would schedule any meeting or appointment.
- Make sure the next session is on your calendar before you quit the one you are currently doing.
- Alternatively, consider making working through this book your "job," spending 2–3 hours on it in the morning and another 2–3 hours in the afternoon for a day or two until it is completed.

Be Accountable

- Tell a friend or two your plan. Send them your schedule.
- Let them know you will report back to them after each session.
- Ask them to "hold your feet to the fire." No excuses!

Find or Form a Group

- See if your local employment office has a workshop based on this book. OR
- Find a few fellow job seekers to work through the book with you. They understand what it's like to be looking and you can support each other in your search.
  - Meet regularly in person or via conference call.
  - Start out by reading the following sections in the chapter, *Get Support:*
    - "Join a Support Group or Create One of Your Own," page 82.
    - "Who Are Your Support People?" page 81.

As you go through this book, you may find ideas that don't work for you. The ideas presented here are suggestions, not mandates. Just because they work for some people, not all of them will work for you. An idea may be usable as-is, might be helpful with some customization, or might not be right for you at all. Knowing yourself and your work style is important. Don't try to force something that doesn't resonate.

If you are collecting unemployment insurance, you will find many ideas in this book that you can use to report for your required weekly job-searching activities. In addition, the job-search action plan you develop, along with dates of completion, will help you keep track of your actions when it's time to do your weekly report.

Job hunting is a job in itself. It's tempting to do anything BUT look for a job when you are unemployed. But you absolutely can be successful. This book will help you plan your search and follow through on that plan. It will help you conquer the avoidance that's your search's worst enemy. You have to be persistent. You have to be flexible. And you have to know how to stay on the task. Make finishing this book your first goal and the rest will become a lot easier.

Taking Stock

Before reading further, please fill out this questionnaire. It will give you a bird's-eye view of where you are now in the search process and where you need to go next.

There's no score to be tallied; there are no right or wrong answers; you don't "pass" or "fail." This is an exercise in self-awareness. The goal here is to give you an overall view of your job search.

For each question, check off as many as apply.

The Job-Search Process

Deciding on a career path

____ I know what I want to do, and I either have or know how to get the qualifications for the jobs I'm looking for.

____ I know what I want to do, but I don't know how to get the qualifications for the jobs I'm looking for.

____ I have some idea of what I am looking for, but need to narrow it down.

____ I have no idea of what kind of job I should be looking for.

Regarding my most recent job

____ I am looking for another job in the same field.

____ I need to change careers because the job opportunities in my field are shrinking.

____ I want to change careers because I no longer want to work in that field.

____ I need to find jobs in new areas that I can transition my skills to.

____ I need to take a new look at my interests, my personality, my skills, and my aptitudes to get an idea of new career paths.

Additional training or education

____ I do not need any additional training or education to get a job in my chosen field.

____ I need additional training or education to get a job in my chosen field.

____ I have spoken to a career counselor or other knowledgeable person who can guide me in finding the right training or education, and (if needed) who can tell me about possible financial aid or scholarships.

The job outlook opportunities in my chosen field

____ Are excellent.

____ Are fair.

____ Are poor. I need to find another field.

____ I have no idea what the outlook is.

Finding support

____ I know many of the kinds of support that are available to me in my job search.

____ I know some of the kinds of support that are available to me in my job search.

____ I have no idea what kinds of support are available to me in my job search.

My résumé

____ Is complete and ready to send.

____ Is in good shape, just needs a few updates.

____ Needs a lot of updates.

____ I've completed a first draft.

____ I have a draft copy started.

____ I haven't even started to write a résumé.

When it comes to my online presence

____ I am careful with my Facebook, Instagram, Twitter, and Snapchat postings. I know potential employers are watching!

____ I am not careful, but my social media accounts are private so hopefully only friends and family can see my postings.

____ Anyone can see anything I post, and I don't worry about who might be reading or what I might be saying.

____ I make sure that all of my online entities are consistent with what I present on paper and what I present in person.

Contacts I can use for networking

____ I need to create a list of people that I can contact.

____ I have a list of people I can contact, but it needs to be updated.

____ I have a complete list of all of the people that I can contact.

People on my contact list

____ I maintain my network, contacting at least two people on the list each week, whether or not I'm looking for a job.

____ I help others on my list and make sure it's not all one-sided.

____ I spend the majority of my one-on-one time strengthening my relationships with people who can make a difference in my search (quality vs. quantity).

____ Some of the people in my network are mentors as well as peers.

____ I always send a thank-you note to anyone who helps me.

Networking via volunteerism

___ When I volunteer, I look for positions that will showcase my talents or will widen my skills.

___ When volunteering, I always show what a good worker I am.

___ I say yes to almost any kind of volunteering, regardless of how it will impact my job search.

Interviewing

___ I do my due diligence in researching the company, the product (if applicable), and if possible, the people with whom I will be speaking (check out their LinkedIn profiles) before my interview.

___ I feel comfortable interviewing and know that I interview well.

___ I feel that I can benefit from interview training.

My LinkedIn profile

___ Is complete and up-to-date.

___ Is probably 50–80% complete and current.

___ Is about 25–50% complete and current.

___ Is less than 25% complete and current.

___ Is just a stub with my name and little else.

___ I don't have a LinkedIn account.

Possible barrier(s) to employment

___ Mature worker

___ Past offender

___ Disability

___ Long time out of the workforce

___ Lack of experience

If I checked off one of the above, I have done the following

___ Looked online for advice from reputable websites.

___ Looked for relevant workshops from my local American Job Center, Vocational Rehabilitation Center, or other career center.

___ Signed up for counseling from my local American Job Center, Vocational Rehabilitation Center, or other career center.

___ Other: _____.

___ Nothing, except for maybe worrying about it.

Overall, on a scale of 1–10, where

> 1 = "My job-search process is in excellent shape" and
>
> 10 = "My job-search process is a disaster,"

I would give myself a rating of: _____.

Your Job-Search Time

When it's time to get started on the job search

____ I get right to it.

____ I sometimes have a hard time getting to it.

____ I often find something that distracts me from sitting down to work.

____ Getting started is a frequent and serious problem for me.

When I begin my job search each day, I first start on

____ Checking my email.

____ Organizing my day.

____ The most urgent task.

____ The hardest task.

____ The easiest task.

____ Whatever catches my eye first.

____ Other: _____ .

When I start my job search each day, I

____ Get right to work on the most appropriate task.

____ Get right to work, but usually not on the task I should be doing first.

____ Plan to get to work, but usually get distracted and do something unrelated.

When I'm done with my search for the day, my job-search space is usually

____ Cleared off, or at least tidy.

____ A disaster.

____ Something in between.

I generally do things that need to be done

____ When they become urgent.

____ When I'm in the right mood or it feels like the right time, but that doesn't work well.

____ When I'm in the right mood or it feels like the right time; it works well for me.

____ In a timely fashion because I plan ahead.

I delegate non-search tasks that are appropriate to be delegated to those who live with me

____ Often.

____ Sometimes.

____ Rarely or never.

____ N/A.

When it comes to promising to do non-search activities, I generally
___ Bite off more than I can chew.
___ Am a good judge of only taking on only what I can accomplish.
___ Avoid taking on any additional tasks because I fear becoming too busy.

Regarding distractions
___ Distractions are a real problem for my productivity.
___ Distractions are somewhat of a problem for my productivity.
___ Distractions aren't a problem for me.

Regarding how I handle interruptions
___ If a friend or family member interrupts me, I usually talk with them even if I'm busy.
___ If a friend or family member interrupts me, I keep it as brief as possible and get back to work.
___ I always answer my desk phone or cell phone when it rings, even if it's not an important call.
___ I check who's calling, then only answer if necessary or convenient.
___ I often welcome distractions, because I'm avoiding what I should be doing.
___ I'm very careful about avoiding distractions.

Regarding working on specific job-search tasks
___ I avoid tasks I don't like.
___ I avoid getting started on big projects.
___ I can have a hard time getting started on things even when I enjoy them.
___ I save the tasks I like least for last, and that works for me.
___ I save the tasks I like least for last, but it's a problem.
___ I do the tasks that need to be done in a timely fashion.
___ Other: _____.

Regarding job-search-related voice mails
___ I return most job-search-related phone calls in a timely manner (within 24 hours).
___ I eventually return most job-search-related phone calls.
___ I rarely return job-search-related phone calls.

Regarding reading email in general
___ I read my email as soon as it lands in my inbox, but that interferes with my job search.
___ I read my email as soon as it lands in my inbox; it's not a problem for me.
___ I check my email a lot; it interferes with my job search.
___ I check my email a lot; it isn't a problem for my productivity.
___ I check my email at a few prescribed times during the day.
___ I check my email once a day.
___ I check my email less than once a day.

Regarding job-search-related emails

___ I return most job-search-related emails as soon as I read them.

___ I return most job-search-related emails within 24 hours.

___ I eventually return job-search-related emails.

___ I rarely return job-search-related emails.

Regarding personal (non-search–related) emails that arrive when I'm working on the job search

___ They are significantly interfering with my productivity.

___ They are somewhat interfering with my productivity.

___ They are not interfering with my productivity.

___ I don't read them while I'm working on the job search.

I feel most energetic and productive

___ In the early morning.

___ Mid-morning to late morning.

___ Right after lunch.

___ Mid-afternoon to late afternoon.

___ Right after dinner.

___ Late at night.

___ Rarely or never. *(Please complete the wellness questionnaire on page 125)*

Regarding your energy levels throughout the day

___ I know when I'm most energetic, and do the hardest or most unpleasant tasks then.

___ I save the easier tasks for my lower-energy periods.

___ I know when I'm most energetic, but rarely take advantage of those times.

___ I have no idea when I'm most energetic, so don't really plan my tasks with that in mind.

If you think you waste too much time when you are working on the job search, what are the biggest problems for you? (Select as many as apply, ranking in order: 1 = worst problem, 2 = second worst problem, and so forth.)

___ Distracted by Internet (personal email, social networking, Web surfing, online games, etc.)

___ Distracted by friends and family members

___ Difficulty sitting still; always finding reasons to get up and move around

___ Distracted by cell phone, texting, etc.

___ Find myself daydreaming, or have a hard time focusing

___ Dislike a lot of the tasks I have to do

___ Sleepiness

___ Other: _____.

I feel like my personal life intrudes on my job-search time

___ Often, and that's fine with me.

___ Often, but I don't like it.

___ Occasionally.

___ Rarely or never.

Overall, on a scale of 1–10, where

1 = "I use my job-search time very productively," and

10 = "I use my job-search time very poorly,"

I would give myself a rating of: _____ .

Your Priorities

Job hunters are among the most creative and productive people I know! They can be enormously creative in finding ways to avoid the job search. They can be highly productive in doing everything in the world that they were going to get to "someday." Closets get cleaned out; rooms get painted; helping others takes on a new importance and urgency. The old saying about others' poor planning changes to, "Your inability to plan absolutely *is* an emergency on my part, and I will be thrilled to help you right now!"

When avoiding the search, job hunters tell themselves that whatever they are doing instead is important. It's easy to equate activity with productivity and energy expenditure with forward progress. But deep down they know they're not really the same thing. AWOL job seekers justify and rationalize everything they do that's not job-search related. But at the end of the day, they go to bed frustrated and feeling bad about themselves and the job search, desperately hoping to do better tomorrow.

Moving Rocks

Consider Fred. Fred had a big pile of rocks in his front yard, which he spent the morning moving to the back yard. He worked quickly to get it all done before noon. After lunch, he spent the afternoon moving the rocks back to their original spot. At the end of the day, he was tired but happy, feeling good about how hard he had worked. What did he accomplish? *Nothing*.

When you are avoiding the job search, you can spend a lot of time "moving rocks." You do it every time you do something that is a lower priority than your job search. If you work hard enough on it, you can fool yourself into thinking you've done something useful. That way, you don't have to feel guilty about not looking for employment.

It's really easy to spend your time on activities that, in the moment, seem to be accomplishing something. And they might indeed be accomplishing *something*, just not what you need to be accomplishing—and that is finding a job. They feel good while you are doing them, but at the end of the day, you're left with guilt and frustration, wondering where the day went.

You can't put your life on hold during your job search. There are definitely things that need to be done that aren't related to finding employment. But you will need to get your priorities straight. "Moving rocks" is just another of the many creative methods we use to avoid staying on task.

This book will provide you with the tools you need to prioritize your job-search activities and your life activities.

The Covey Quadrants

According to Stephen Covey, in his landmark book, *The 7 Habits of Highly Effective People*,[1] every activity you do can be classified into one of four categories or quadrants:

	Urgent	Not Urgent
Important	**Quadrant I** Examples: • Items with an imminent deadline • Unexpected emergencies • Last-minute changes	**Quadrant II** Examples: • Completing your résumé • Researching companies • Working on items with a long deadline
Not Important	**Quadrant III** Examples: • Other peoples' problems • Interruptions • Whatever is in front of your nose	**Quadrant IV** Examples: • YouTube • Social media • Computer games

Quadrant I: Urgent and Important

Quadrant I activities have an imminent deadline. Working on them can be stressful and overwhelming. If you spend the majority of your time working under the gun on urgent and important tasks, you could be headed for burnout. We all have to spend some time in Quadrant I, as life has a way of throwing us the unexpected. But devoting more time to Quadrant II activities can keep you out of Quadrant I by preventing last-minute crises, thus reducing your overall level of stress, and increasing your efficiency and effectiveness.

Quadrant II: Important but Not Urgent

These activities fall into two subcategories: those with a deadline but plenty of time to complete, and those with no deadline. The latter are things that are the easiest to avoid, but by doing so you really sabotage yourself. I've worked with clients who have been unemployed for months, but have yet to get their résumé updated. Calling headhunters, making a list of target companies, and getting some additional training are all important activities you can avoid forever. But if you don't do them, you'll find yourself unemployed forever.

Quadrant III: Urgent but Not Important

We can really fool ourselves into thinking things are important just because they *appear* to be urgent. Often, what's in front of our face can seem terribly important. We see something we've been planning to get to for ages, and suddenly think, "Maybe I'll do this right now while I'm thinking about it." Thinking about it makes it feel urgent, and not wanting to work on the job search makes it feel important. I once had a client tell me that she went to get something out of her closet that was relevant to her task at hand, and while she was there she decided to dust the closet!

Quadrant IV: Not Important and Not Urgent

Another name for Quadrant IV is Time Wasters. There are zillions of them. The Internet is a particularly seductive one, especially since you have to spend so much time on it in searching for a job. YouTube, Facebook, and Twitter are not your friends when you need to be focusing on the job search.

That said, spending some time vegging in Quadrant IV can be useful and (ironically) *important* when you're burned out and need a break. But when time wasters are taking over your life, I call them "black holes." Being aware of your personal black holes and knowing how they affect your productivity can be very helpful in managing them.

Exercises

Quadrant I (Urgent and Important): Do you have any upcoming deadlines for your job search? If so, what are they and when are the deadlines?

Activity:_____ Date due:_____

Activity:_____ Date due:_____

Activity:_____ Date due:_____

Quadrant II (Important but Not Urgent): What are activities that either have a distant deadline or no deadline, but are vital for finding a job? As you list each one, score it as follows:

    1 = I'm on top of it; it's coming along well.

    2 = It's getting there but not as fast as I would like.

    3 = It's really stalled; I'd rather be cleaning the toilet than working on it.

Activity:_____ Score:_____

Activity:_____ Score:_____

Activity:_____ Score:_____

Quadrant III (Urgent but Not Important): What are the activities that you typically do that feel urgent and seem important in the moment, but afterwards you realize they were not a good use of your time?

Activity:_____

Activity:_____

Activity:_____

Quadrant IV (Not Important and Not Urgent): What sorts of things do you do that distract you from your job search?

Activity:_____

Activity:_____

Activity:_____

Moving Rocks: What are some of the ways you fool yourself in the moment, thinking that you are being productive, but in reality accomplish nothing?

Activity:_____

Activity:_____

Activity:_____

The majority of this book will be devoted to keeping you working on the things that you need to do that are important but not urgent. If you are stopping now, make sure you've entered into your calendar the date and time of your next session.

Part Two:

Strategies for Staying On Task

Avoid Your Personal Black Holes

A black hole is a region in space that has so much mass that nothing, not even light, can escape. Black holes are great metaphors for activities that draw us in so strongly that once we start doing them, we just can't seem to escape and get back to work. Covey Quadrant IV activities (not important or urgent) can often be black holes.

LinkedIn? Or SuckedIn?

Used well, LinkedIn is a powerful tool for the job search.
Your profile needs to be in tip-top shape. You can use it to follow your target companies or work on expanding your first-degree network. You can learn about a prospective hiring manager with whom you have an interview coming up. Or you can take part in a group that is relevant to your chosen industry.

But you can also waste a lot of time on LinkedIn—telling yourself that since it's LinkedIn, you are still working on your job search, right? Wrong-o! How much time do you spend in groups that aren't going to be helpful to you? When you are in a group that sounds interesting, do you find yourself clicking on items that are enticing even though they have no relationship to the job you are looking for and won't advance your goals?

Most black holes aren't so subtle. There's no doubt that when you're playing computer games, checking sports scores, or watching YouTube, you are not advancing your quest for employment. What's hard is that so much job-search work needs to be done on the computer and all of those seductive websites are just a click away.

BIG NATE ©2017 Lincoln Peirce. Reprinted by permission of ANDREWS MCMEEL SYNDICATION for UFS. All rights reserved.

It's not always obvious when something is a black hole. If it's easy for you to limit an activity, it's probably not a black hole. The question is, are you controlling the activity or is it controlling you? Black holes for most people are addictive. There's just no stopping once they get started. No matter what your black-hole-of-choice is, when you indulge it's next to impossible to get back on track.

Are You Enjoying or Avoiding?

While we may enjoy most of the activities that are our black holes, there are some that we engage in not because we enjoy them, but because we are actively avoiding something else. Or sometimes it's too much trouble to go back to what we need to be doing. For example, once your favorite TV program is over, do you channel-surf until you find the least awful option to watch, rather than getting back to work (or in the evening, going to bed to get a good night's sleep)?

Case Study: Coffee and the Morning Paper

I worked with a client who would start his day with the newspaper and a cup of coffee. He'd read everything of interest while he drank his coffee. Then he'd get a second cup, which he didn't really want, and waste time reading things of no real interest. As a result, his day would start much later than he liked.

He estimated that it took him about 45 minutes to read the things he cared about, so we agreed he would set the timer to limit the reading to that time period. In many cases, setting the timer to limit an activity is sufficient, and he thought that would work. However, the next week, when I asked him how it went, he reported that the plan had failed. The newspaper was a black hole for him; it was controlling his morning. I suggested that he put off reading the paper until the evening, and he was okay with that. The information he was getting from it was not nearly as significant as the amount of time he was wasting with it.

Case Study: Online Games

Another client of mine would take her iPad to bed with her, intending to wind down with an e-book, but instead staying up very late playing *Words With Friends* and missing sleep. She stopped taking the iPad upstairs with her at night. Instead, she went back to reading good old-fashioned books in bed, and that solved the problem. Sometimes physical separation is the best approach to avoiding something that we have trouble controlling.

It's okay to indulge in activities that you enjoy that are black holes. Just be sure to schedule them at an appropriate time. You can even use your black hole as a reward for having accomplished a goal. However, beware—indulging in a black hole at the end of the day can result in missed sleep, as you stay up all hours of the night enjoying your black-hole activity. Better to schedule it as a leisure activity to enjoy on a day off.

Summary

Now that you're aware of black holes, be wary of them. Sometimes you need to relax with something mindless. But if you find you're often wasting time with a particular activity when you should be working on your job search, or you feel the activity is controlling you, it's probably a black hole sucking you in. You might need to plan a specific time to enjoy it.
In some cases, you might need to stay away from it altogether, cold-turkey. If it's an app, you might need to delete it from your phone, tablet, or computer. If your black hole is a portable electronic device, put it in a remote spot in your house during times you are vulnerable so that it will take effort to retrieve it.

Exercise

Think about what your personal black holes are when it comes to your job search, and list two of them in the first column of the chart on the next page. Then fill out the rest of the chart for each one. Note that your black holes may be some of the same activities you identified in Covey Quadrant IV (not important or urgent).

If you are going to take a break now, be sure to schedule your next session with this book.

BLACK HOLE	HOW MUCH DO I ENJOY THIS BLACK HOLE?	HOW MUCH DOES IT INTERFERE WITH ACHIEVING MY GOALS?	HOW MUCH DOES IT CONTROL ME?	DO I DIVE INTO THIS BLACK HOLE BECAUSE I ENJOY IT, OR TO AVOID THINGS?	IS THIS BLACK HOLE OK SOMETIMES, OR SHOULD I AVOID IT COMPLETELY?	WHAT IS MY PLAN FOR DEALING WITH THIS BLACK HOLE?
	___ A lot ___ Fair amount ___ Somewhat ___ A little ___ Very little ___ Not at all	___ A lot ___ Fair amount ___ Somewhat ___ A little ___ Very little ___ Not at all	___ A lot ___ Fair amount ___ Somewhat ___ A little ___ Very little ___ Not at all	___ Always because I enjoy it ___ Usually because I enjoy it ___ 50/50 ___ Usually for avoidance ___ Always for avoidance	___ I can do it occasionally ___ I can do it occasionally, but only if I plan how much I'll do ahead of time ___ I should avoid it completely	
	___ A lot ___ Fair amount ___ Somewhat ___ A little ___ Very little ___ Not at all	___ A lot ___ Fair amount ___ Somewhat ___ A little ___ Very little ___ Not at all	___ A lot ___ Fair amount ___ Somewhat ___ A little ___ Very little ___ Not at all	___ Always because I enjoy it ___ Usually because I enjoy it ___ 50/50 ___ Usually for avoidance ___ Always for avoidance	___ I can do it occasionally ___ I can do it occasionally, but only if I plan how much I'll do ahead of time ___ I should avoid it completely	

Deal with Distractions

When you're working on the job search, distractions can slow you down or derail you altogether. And if what you're doing is something you don't particularly enjoy, those distractions can be really enticing. To deal with them effectively, it helps if you can anticipate what they'll be ahead of time, then modify your environment to keep them to a minimum. Implementing the ideas in this chapter before you start a task can reduce the number of distractions you will have to fend off. Ben Franklin was right: "An ounce of prevention is worth a pound of cure." Here are some strategies to help prevent distractions while you are working.

Ignore the E-Temptation

It's almost impossible these days to conduct an effective job search without the Internet. Whether you're researching a company on LinkedIn or taking an online course to update your skills, fun and interesting websites are beckoning. No matter how firm your resolve to ignore them, sometimes their siren song is just too strong.

Fortunately, there are apps and add-ons that you can install to keep you on the straight and narrow while you're on your computer. Here are two that are available for Google Chrome:

- **Strict Workflow:**[2] Forces 25 minutes of distraction-free work followed by a 5-minute break. Allows you to blacklist distracting sites during the work period.
- **Stay Focused:**[3] Increases your productivity by limiting the amount of time you can spend on time-wasting websites.

For smartphones, **Forest**[4] is fun app that helps you stay focused by planting a tree when you start a task. The tree grows as long as you stay in the Forest app, but it dies if you leave the app before your allotted time is up.

You can learn more about these and similar apps and add-ons by searching for "Internet focus apps." But be careful to limit the amount of time you search!

Social Media

Before you start a task, log out of Facebook and any other social media that might tempt you. And turn off Twitter! You don't even have to go searching for Tweets; they come searching for you and like so many other things they are very, very seductive.

Close Your Email (Gasp!)

Very few emails need a response immediately. Seeing a new email come in is a really tempting distraction, especially if what you're doing is difficult or you're not enjoying it. If you don't close your email program, at least turn off the "new email" notification signal. It's good to make it a policy to check email only at pre-planned intervals throughout the day, or at the end of an uninterrupted period of work.

Deal with Loved Ones

The people you live with can be the biggest impediments to finding a job. Your family, if you have one, wants to be helpful and supportive and probably has a vested interest in your becoming employed. However they can also be a major source of interruptions, especially if they are home with you. "Bill, can you pick up Jerry from his piano lesson?" "Emily, we're out of milk and I need it to make dinner." "Hey, can you lend me a hand with this?"

While they don't mean to distract you, it may feel to them like you have all the time in the world. But the truth is that finding a job IS a job in and of itself. To be successful, you need to restrict your availability. So set the stage when you want a chunk of uninterrupted time:

- **The Day Before:** State your intentions. "I want to work on my job search from 9 until noon tomorrow. Is there anything scheduled for that time which can be done now instead, or put off until tomorrow afternoon?"
- **The Day Of:** Remind your loved one of your plan. "Just wanted to remind you that I want to work on my job search until noon. Once I start, I really need to focus. Is there anything we need to address beforehand?"
- **Right Before You Start:** Announce that you are starting your work and that you'll check in at noon when you are done.

Okay, so you've laid the groundwork for a nice uninterrupted chunk of fruitful work. But 10 minutes after you start, there's a good chance your spouse or partner will call, or knock, or find some other way to intrude without even realizing it. It's not that they're stupid or thoughtless or trying to sabotage your plans. It's just that they are preoccupied with what's happening in their own lives and, like most everyone else on the planet, it's easy for them to forget the plan.

You may want to agree on some sort of visual reminder that will stop the interruption before it happens. You can put a "Do Not Disturb" sign on your door or on the back of your chair. I had a client once who draped crime scene tape in a visible place when she didn't want to be disturbed. To prevent untimely phone calls, let people know that you won't answer the phone unless they call twice within a minute or so—and they should only do that when it's truly urgent.

Teach Children to Wait

If you're working at home around your children, they can be taught to wait their age in minutes. When your four-year-old wants your attention, set a timer for four minutes and tell him that he will have to wait until the timer goes off. Be fair; when the four minutes is up, attend to the child's need. Doing this teaches your child both patience and respect for others' time.

Better yet, find someone who can occupy your children's time. When I had young children and was working from home, I found a neighboring homeschooler who could play with my kids at my house. She was too young to be left alone in the house with them, so her services were less expensive than daycare or an older babysitter. I've found most homeschoolers to be quite mature and responsible. If you don't know any homeschoolers yourself, search for a homeschooling support group in your area or ask around for referrals of trustworthy neighborhood kids.

Another possibility, if you know someone else with young children at home, is to swap babysitting time with them or join a babysitting co-op. But remember, for every hour someone else watches your children, you'll have to pay that hour back.

Leave Home

Sometimes searching for a job from home is just too difficult. There are too many chores, people, and other distractions beckoning. If that happens, take your job search elsewhere. Your local library can be a great place to work. You can commandeer a quiet table and totally focus on the task at hand. Reference librarians can provide suggestions for job-search resources and some libraries also sponsor meetings for job seekers.

Often, career centers offer places you can sit and work on your search. Coffee shops with WiFi service ("Internet cafes") are also a good choice if you work well in places that have some activity going on. Some people concentrate better with a bit of background noise; for others it's a distraction.

Ignore Your Phone

Don't answer the phone (landline or cell), or even better turn the ringer off. If you can't do this, decide ahead of time whose calls you will answer. You probably want to pick it up if it's your child's school, the doctor, or a hiring manager or headhunter. But beware of friends and relatives who just call to chat—save that for later.

Silence texting notifications also. Texting is a huge distraction in many lives today. We're becoming "online all the time" and hence infinitely interruptible. We can't work efficiently when we're constantly stopping to read and send texts. Few texts demand immediate attention anyway.

Plan Ahead

Get your coffee or tea before you start and gather everything you need for the task at hand. Having to stop to get things can really slow you down.

Get Comfortable

Make sure you're as comfortable as possible before you start. Being uncomfortable can be a significant distraction. Is your chair at a comfortable height? If you can control the temperature, is the room either too hot or too cold? What else do you need to do to make sure that you are comfortable while you work?

But Not Too Comfortable!

Most people are more focused if they sit upright, rather than slouching or working in an easy chair. Some people even find they are more productive when they work standing up.

Set a Timer

Finally, set a timer for a specific period of time and do not succumb to the temptation of interruptions before it goes off. It's amazing how much easier it is to avoid getting distracted when you focus yourself for a specific period of time with a timer. You know that when it rings, you can deal with those other things in your life; you aren't putting them off indefinitely. Alternatively, instead of using a timer, you can pick a whole-number goal like "make three phone calls."

Summary

The secret to dealing with distractions is to anticipate and plan ahead for them. Forewarned is forearmed! Before you start working, think of the ways that interruptions typically happen for you. Then set up your environment to minimize the chances they will occur. Also, think about how to deal with distractions if they do happen despite your best efforts to avoid them.

Exercise

Think of three distractions that might occur during your job search. In the table on the next page, write down each one and how you could decrease the chances of it happening. Finally, write down how you could deal with the distraction to minimize its impact if it occurs.

Possible Distraction	How to Prevent or Decrease Odds of It Occurring	How to Deal with It If It Does Occur

The next two chapters will take some time to complete. You will be creating a complete job-search action plan and a schedule to carry it out. It's ideal to complete that in one sitting if possible so this might be a good time to take a break. Be sure to decide when you are going to return and note it on your calendar.

Part Three:

Creating a Master Plan and Schedule

Create a Job-Search Action Plan

An effective job search has a lot of moving parts. It's essential to approach this with an organized, well-thought-out plan of attack. Inefficiency can lead to delays in finding the right job. Rather than wasting time with Quadrant III (urgent, not important) and Quadrant IV (not urgent, not important) activities, concentrate your efforts on Quadrant II (not urgent, important) activities that keep you on task and on schedule.

In this chapter, you will create your job-search action plan—a list of all of the actions necessary for a thorough and effective approach to finding a job.

Start by Choosing the Tasks

The following is a comprehensive list of ideas for job seekers. Go through the list and check off all of the tasks that you know you will have to complete to do an effective, thorough, and efficient search. Place an "O" in front of tasks that are optional, those that may enhance your search but aren't as important. Leave blank any activities that you know won't work for you or that you have already done.

Please note this is a very extensive list. Be realistic about the number of items you choose to incorporate into your job-search action plan. Do not check off more than you can reasonably do.

One-Time Tasks

Career path

___ Complete the *Labor Market Information Research Worksheet* (Appendix G) to confirm that there are realistic hiring prospects for my desired position.

___ Confirm whether or not I currently have the background for my desired position.

___ If I don't have the needed background, determine what I need to do to get it.

___ Find out what other positions I might be qualified for.

___ Decide on the job sector(s) I want to work in.

___ Assess my skills that might transfer to other types of jobs.

___ Consider my personal branding. ("What do I bring to the party that is unique?")

Support

___ Find career centers in my area. (See Appendix C—*What Are American Job Centers?*—for more information.)

___ Explore services offered by my local career center.

___ Register for relevant workshops and services offered by my local career center.

___ Sign up for assessments as needed:
    ___ Skill levels
    ___ Aptitudes
    ___ Interests
    ___ Abilities
    ___ Myers-Briggs
    ___ Other: _____

___ Look for counseling, articles, and workshops that address my concerns about age, having a criminal record, long gap in employment history, disability, or other perceived barrier(s) to employment.

___ Look for professional recruiters ("headhunters") who place candidates in my field.

___ Join or create a support group of job seekers that meets regularly.

___ Explore the possibility of working with a private career coach, life coach, or ADHD (attention deficit/hyperactivity disorder) coach.

Unemployment Insurance benefits

___ Determine if I'm eligible for unemployment benefits *(if not, skip to "Résumé, etc.")*.

___ Find out what it takes to meet my state's requirements.

___ Apply for unemployment insurance benefits.

___ Decide on a way to keep track of job actions that satisfy the weekly check-in requirement.

Résumé, etc.

___ Create or update a customizable master résumé.

___ Sign up for a résumé workshop or make an appointment with a résumé consultant to go over my résumé.

___ Create a master cover letter that I can customize for each job I apply to.

___ Ask 2–3 people to be references for me before I apply to any jobs.

Networking

___ Create a list of all of the people that I can contact, including their names, contact information, and my connection to them.

___ Volunteer as a way to widen my network, learn new skills, and give back.

___ Join relevant industry groups and professional organizations.

___ Create a website about my professional self.

___ Print business cards with my name, contact information, and areas of expertise.

LinkedIn

___ Take a class at a local career center, American Job Center, or online to learn more about using LinkedIn.

___ Complete my profile. Make sure it is current and well-written.

___ Join groups that are relevant to my career goals.

___ Write *sincere* recommendations for former supervisors, co-workers, clients, and other professional contacts.

___ Request former supervisors, co-workers, clients, and other professional contacts give me recommendations and endorsements.

___ Check my skills list and make sure it aligns with the skills needed for my desired job.

___ Prune any skills from my list that aren't relevant to my search.

Online research

___ Create a list of job boards that I want to search regularly. (See Appendix F—*Online Job Boards*—for ideas.)

___ Make a list of target companies that I would like to work for and keep track of their openings.

___ Create an O*NET OnLine account at *https://www.onetonline.org*.

___ Check out my state's online job resources.

Interviewing

___ Explore places where I can get training and feedback to polish my skills.

___ Sign up for an interviewing workshop or coaching.

___ Join Toastmasters to learn to think on my feet and present myself well. (See page 103.)

___ If I was fired, have a good (and honest) response for the question, "Why did you leave your previous position?"

___ Be prepared to answer other hard questions about myself that may come up in an interview.

___ Prepare quantifiable results to discuss during an interview (e.g., instead of, "I always exceeded my sales goals," be prepared to say, "I consistently exceeded my weekly sales goals by 10–20%. I did that by…").

Education/Training

___ Research the kinds of training, classes, or education needed for my career goals.

___ Find institutions that offer the education/training I need for my career goals.

___ Apply for education/training classes.

___ Research financial aid.

___ Brush up or learn new computer skills with online or in-person classes.

Dealing with a Disability

___ Find vocational rehabilitation centers in my area. (See Appendix D—*What Are Vocational Rehabilitation Centers?*—for more information.)

___ Explore services offered by my local Vocational Rehabilitation Center (VRC).

___ Register for relevant workshops and services offered by my local VRC.

___ Sign up for assessments as needed.

___ Learn about adaptive technology that might be needed to do my job.

___ Know what accommodations might be needed for me to do my desired job.

Other

___ _____

___ _____

___ _____

___ _____

Schedule Regularly

Unemployment Insurance benefits

___ Do the weekly mandatory online or in-person check-in.

Networking

___ Contact at least ___ people on my list each week and make notes about each contact.

___ Participate in relevant networking groups online, including LinkedIn, Facebook, and Twitter, ___ times each week.

___ Participate in online discussion boards and email groups relevant to my professional interests ___ times each week.

___ Set up informational interviews with people who have a position I aspire to.

___ Attend industry group and professional organization functions to meet people face-to-face.

___ Attend networking meetings for fellow job seekers.

___ Attend social events that will expose me to new people to widen my network.

LinkedIn

___ Comment on or initiate updates, shares, posts, and group conversations ___ times a week to keep my exposure high.

___ Search for job openings on LinkedIn using the Advanced Search Option.

___ Invite additional connections, especially with people who might work for prospective employers.

Online research

___ Look for job fairs and other hiring events.

Other

___ _____
___ _____
___ _____
___ _____

Schedule As Needed

Networking
___ Ask people in my network for an introduction to someone in a position to hire me.
___ Write a thank-you note or email to anyone who helps me in my job search.

Online research
___ Check out commuting logistics for desired positions.

Interviewing
___ Use LinkedIn, Glassdoor, and other relevant websites to learn about a company before any interviews.
___ Write a thank-you note or email to anyone who interviewed me.

Other

___ _____
___ _____
___ _____
___ _____

The First Draft is Complete

You now have chosen the steps that you need to be doing to land that next job as quickly and efficiently as possible. As you proceed with your search, you will probably make modifications to this job-search action plan. But this gets you started and gives you an idea of all of the things you need to do to get back in the workforce.

Next, we will create a timeline to make sure that all of your job-search action plan tasks are scheduled. This will take about an hour and you will first need to assemble some materials. If you can commit the time now, please move on to the next chapter. If you are going to assemble the materials and make your timeline later, be sure to decide when you are going to do it and schedule it on your calendar.

The 10,000-Foot Perspective

How quickly do you need to find a job? If you are collecting unemployment insurance, you typically have 26 weeks of benefits. That might seem like a lot of time—what's the hurry, you ask yourself? Okay, maybe you need a week or two to take a break, get your feet under you, and psychologically gear up for the search. But the truth is, there really is a LOT you need to do to conduct a thorough and effective job search—as seen in the job-search action plan you just created! Without a comprehensive overall timetable those weeks will pass before you know it.

If you only plan week-to-week, you can end up jammed against deadlines and put yourself in financial and psychological jeopardy. It's important to step back and get a bird's-eye view of the search from start to finish. Then, you need to keep that view in front of you.

Old-Fashioned vs. Newfangled

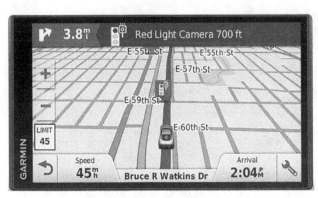

Copyright 2018 Garmin LTD or its Subsidiaries. All Rights Reserved.

If you use a Global Positioning System (GPS), you know how easily it can get you from Point A to Point B. The problem is that it gives you no overall perspective. You might reach your destination without having any idea of how you got there or even where your destination is. It's difficult to see your progress, get an idea of how far you've come, or truly see how far you have to go, other than knowing you have a certain number of miles and time to travel before reaching your destination.

A map, on the other hand, gives you a bird's-eye view of your world. You can see the whole trip in one glance. As you go along, you know exactly how far you've come and exactly how far you have to go to get to your destination. It gives you perspective.

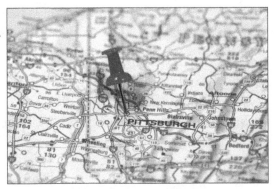

We are going to create a map of your job search. In this chapter you will create a 12-week plan called a "timetable wall" that will enable you to see your whole search, and everything you have yet to do.

Create a Timetable Wall

Creating a master timetable wall (in the "old technology," hands-on style) will give you a realistic view of what you need to do, and how much time you have to accomplish it. It will bring the future into the present instead of its seeming very far away—out there somewhere on the horizon. It will be a map view instead of a GPS view.

Materials needed:
- 12 sheets of brightly-colored 8½ × 11 paper
- Scissors
- A stick of "<u>restickable</u>" glue.[†] It is *very* important that the glue is not permanent!
- Pen or fine-tipped marker
- The pages in Appendix H
- A large blank wall—or a loose-leaf notebook if you don't have the wall space

Directions

Create the Weekly Sheets

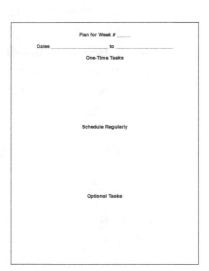

1. Take your 12 colored sheets and write at the top of each:[‡]

     Plan For Week #____
     Dates _____ to _____
     One-Time Tasks

2. One third of the way down, write:

     Schedule Regularly

3. Two thirds of the way down, write:

     Optional Tasks

4. Fill in the week numbers and dates for each sheet.

---

† Typical brands are Scotch Restickable Glue Sticks and Elmer's CraftBond Repositional Glue Sticks.

‡ Copies are available on my website at *JSthatJS.com/Downloads*. Click on "Download Timetable Form."

Schedule One-Time Tasks

1. Remove the first two pages of Appendix H, *One-Time Tasks*, (pages 153 & 155) from the back of this book.
2. Write a ✔ on each task you checked off in your job-search action plan, and an "**O**" on each task you marked as optional.
3. Cut out each task that has a ✔ or an "**O**."
4. Decide what week you want to do each of the tasks.
5. Using restickable glue, affix each task onto the week you're planning to do it:
   a. Tasks with a ✔ go below "One-Time Tasks."
   b. Tasks with "**O**" go below "Optional Tasks."

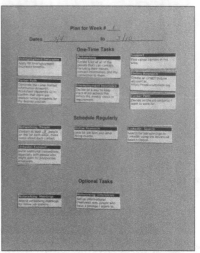

Schedule Repetitive Tasks

1. Remove the next five pages of Appendix H, *Schedule Regularly*, (pages 157–165) from the back of this book.
2. Write a ✔ on each task you checked off in your job-search action plan, and an "**O**" on each task you marked as optional.
3. Cut out each task that has a ✔ or an "**O**."
4. Decide how often you want to do each task and which weeks you want to schedule them.
5. Using restickable glue, affix each task onto the week you're planning to do it:
   a. Tasks with a ✔ go below "Schedule Regularly."
   b. Tasks with "**O**" go below "Optional Tasks."

Schedule as Needed Tasks

1. Remove the last two pages of Appendix H, *Schedule as Needed*, (pages 167 & 169) from the back of this book.
2. Write a ✔ on each task that you checked off in your job-search action plan, and an "**O**" on each task you marked as optional.
3. Affix these onto the weekly sheets as they are appropriate to schedule.

You have now created a complete master timetable for your job search. Of course, most of the things that you need to do to get ready for the search will be clustered in the first weeks of the search. After that, it will mainly consist of repetitive items that you'll need to do each week.

If you have the wall space to hold all of your pages, place them all on that wall, including the "Schedule as Needed" page. This will truly give you the map perspective of all that lies ahead. If you don't have the wall space, you can place each sheet in the loose-leaf notebook. However, a wall is much more effective if you can possibly make it work!

Using the Timetable Wall

You'll be using each sheet on the timetable wall to plan your weeks. As you complete each task, discard its label. On the occasion you don't complete a non-optional task on the week you'd planned to do it, remove it and place it on a different week. If you find you're avoiding, you'll get a visual reminder of the cost of procrastination as unfinished tasks pile up. You don't need to move the unfinished tasks under the "Optional" heading.

This visual representation—being able to see everything at once, both your progress and what lies ahead—is a highly effective aid to keeping you on track. This tool keeps the future before your eyes and makes sure you are aware of the reality of the passing time. It's superior to using the computer or smartphone for your plan because, like a GPS, a screen only allows you to see one small segment of your job-search journey instead of showing you the entire view at once. If you have an app that you absolutely know works for you and will keep you on track, that's fine, but be wary. The visual representation of time can be very powerful.

The next six chapters will give you strategies you can use in carrying out your job search:
- Break down any overwhelming or distasteful tasks into smaller pieces.
- Assign whole-number goals to each task.
- Create new routines.
- Start with small, non-intimidating goals if you are feeling anxious, depressed, or avoidant.
- Create simple reward systems to keep you motivated.
- Decide whether or not you are truly *committing* to doing the task.

Then we will start actually planning how you are going to spend your days and weeks. If you are stopping now, when will you get started again? Be sure to schedule it.

Part Four:

Strategies for Planning Your Week

Break Your Tasks Down into Manageable Pieces

Now you have a list of all of the actions you need to complete to find your job, and a timetable for when you are going to do each one. However, you might find that some of the tasks seem huge and overwhelming.

The best way to approach the large and overwhelming tasks on your job-search action plan is to break down each one into a series of smaller, more manageable pieces. Divide and conquer! By focusing on each piece one at a time, you can make progress without ending up feeling overwhelmed by the whole thing.

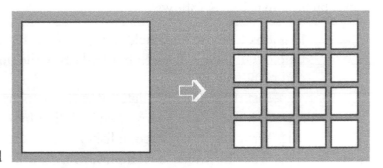

Make sure that each piece in your action plan is small enough to be self-contained, is not overwhelming, and can be completed in one sitting. The result will be a practical and doable plan.

Example: Your Résumé

The item in the job-search action plan states, "Create or update a customizable master résumé." That's a pretty big, amorphous lump. So let's break it down into several sub-steps:

1. Gather the needed data to create or update résumé.
2. Create a first draft.
3. Review the résumé.
4. Create final wording.
5. Choose a résumé format.
6. Create the final version.

If you look at Appendix E, *Résumé Worksheet*, you'll see that step 1 is already broken down further for you:

1. Gather the needed data to create or update résumé.
   a. Write down my contact information.

b. Summarize my professional qualifications.

c. List jobs that I have held in the past 10–15 years, including company name, dates employed, location, and job title. Then write down my key accomplishments and responsibilities.

d. Write down the name and locations of the institutions I attended, the degree or certification conferred upon me, and my major and minor courses of study.

e. Summarize related volunteer experience.

f. List any professional credentials I have.

If any of the above tasks still feel daunting, you can break them down further. For example, you could break down 1.c. as follows:

c. List jobs that you have held in the past 10–15 years, including company name, dates employed, location, and job title. Then write down your key accomplishments and responsibilities.

i. List the names and dates of each company.

ii. List the dates employed and job title for each.

iii. Write down key accomplishments for the first company.

iv. Write down key accomplishments for the second company.

v. Etc.

Taking this approach changes the task from a big looming monster into a set of discrete and manageable steps. Almost any task can be broken down like this into as many levels of sub-tasks as needed. The more onerous the task, the more levels and sub-tasks you might need. In the end, each task should be small enough that you can do it in one session without feeling overwhelmed or avoidant. Each item on the list should feel self-contained, non-intimidating, and very doable.

Refining the Job-Search Action Plan

Break down any of the overwhelming tasks in your job-search action plan into smaller action steps, as needed. You might want to do this exercise on a computer so that you can insert the sub-steps between the larger tasks like I did above. If you think better with paper and pencil, you can get started by writing down each step you want to break down at the top of a separate page in a spiral notebook.

Here are the steps for breaking down your job-search action plan:

1. Going down the list of the items in the first week's plan, find the first one that feels large or complex and break it down into several steps.

2. Look at each of the steps you have created. Which ones need to be further broken down into sub-steps? If a step feels overwhelming or intimidating, it needs to be split up into smaller steps.

3. There is no minimum or maximum to the number of levels of sub-steps you will need to create for each task. If the task looks manageable, you're done. If not, you still have work to do to break it down further.
4. Repeat steps 1–3 for each until you have broken down every overwhelming item planned for the upcoming week into doable chunks.

You can choose to do this for all of the overwhelming tasks in your entire plan, or you can do it weekly as you plan your tasks for the upcoming week.

There are no exercises in this chapter since you will need to break things down as you plan your weeks. Before we do that, the next chapters will give you some more strategies for weekly planning. If you are not moving on to the next chapter now, schedule a time when you will return to the workbook.

Set a Whole-Number Goal

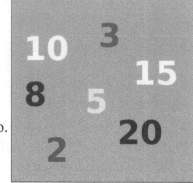

"I really need to just sit down and do it, but I can't seem to get started." That's a refrain I've heard more than once from clients who are stuck in their job search. Hopefully as you plan your week, you'll be able to break down your large job-search activities into a set of distinct, specific tasks. But after that, if you are still struggling to get going, you need to create what I call a whole-number goal. It's simple and takes less than 10 seconds to do.

Before you start your task, all you need to do is decide how much you want to accomplish in one sitting. Deciding on a specific amount that you are going to do makes the task closed-ended, and less overwhelming.

For example, you might choose to:

- Write emails to three people on your contact list.
- Find and schedule two networking events to attend over the next month.
- Send out one LinkedIn invitation.

Or, using the résumé writing example in the previous chapter, you can change "Summarize my professional qualifications" to "Make a list of two of my professional qualifications."

Sometimes the easiest way to set a whole-number goal is to decide on a specific amount of time to work. When procrastination happens, a simple digital timer[†] can be your best ally in getting started. You can use the timer to get yourself going while limiting your commitment to the activity. Setting your timer for a specific amount of time can make the activity feel less daunting. Even if it is a task you find distasteful, you know that the timer will go off and you can stop.

For example, perhaps you are afraid that it might be hard to think of two professional qualifications. You could set the timer for 10 minutes and quit at the end even if you haven't thought of two things when the timer goes off. Then you can come back to it another time.

---

† I strongly recommend NOT using the timer on your cell phone. There are too many other distractions that can ensnare you on phones, especially smartphones.

If you are someone who does not like the idea of breaking down a project like your résumé into all of the discrete units shown in the previous chapter, you can still use the timer to help you get going. If you are avoiding filling out the résumé worksheet in Appendix E, you can set a timer and work on it for a specific amount of time, even as little as five or ten minutes if you are really having a hard time starting.

When you have a job interview coming up and find yourself procrastinating about researching the company, decide on a length of time to do some research, set your timer, and get started.

When you arrive at your goal—whether measured in units or minutes—you can quit for now, knowing you have made progress. Or, if you feel like it, you can set another goal and keep going. There are times that I spend several hours on a project by working in 20-minute chunks and continually resetting the timer. Having a time-limited goal makes it easier to get started, and knowing I can quit when the timer goes off keeps me from succumbing to the urge to stop. Sometimes I get so involved in my task that when the timer beeps, I just turn it off and keep going. Creating a tolerable goal helps me overcome inertia and get started.

No Interruptions Until Finished

Once you get started on your whole-number goal, vow not to let anything distract you. Instead, focus completely on the task. Don't check email, don't stop to get a cup of coffee, don't read or respond to a text. Those things that are trying to distract you will still be there when you complete your goal.

Visualize a barrier

Before you start, it may help to think of an imaginary barrier that will remain in place until you're done. For example, if you are working at your desk, think about how your body feels where it contacts the chair, and then imagine that this contact can't be broken until you get to your goal.

Case Study: *The Joy of Getting Things Done* Newsletter

Even though I enjoy writing, when I sit down to start writing my newsletter, it can be daunting to stare at a blank page. I'm tempted to let anything distract me. But setting the timer for 20 minutes, and knowing I can quit when it beeps, both gets me going and keeps me focused.

Taking Breaks

When you're working on something that's intense or tiring, it's important to take breaks. However, it can be easy to get lost during a break, especially if the task is something you don't particularly enjoy. By setting a timer to limit the break, you can keep it from expanding into wasted time. I suggest positioning the timer far enough away from where you are sitting that you have to actually stand up to turn it off. Otherwise you might hit the "off" button  without even realizing it. Also, use a timer that doesn't stop beeping until you turn it off. Sometimes it takes a while for the beep to penetrate your brain—and if you know the timer will turn itself off, it will be tempting to ignore it.

Limiting Activities

There are a number of job-search activities that need to be done but can suck you in. Before you know it, hours have gone by.

Take email for example. We all have to check it occasionally, but if we're not careful we can waste a lot of time looking at, and passing along, anything funny or clicking on links we don't even care about. I had a client who had this problem until she started setting the timer to limit how long she would spend on her email. That made her focus on the important emails and skip the time wasters.

Taking Too Long on a Task

Sometimes it's easy to spend more time on a task than it really deserves. "Analysis paralysis" can slow progress to a crawl, or even halt it completely. Setting a timer to limit the time you spend on it can help you work quickly and efficiently, without getting bogged down on unimportant details.

Summary

Using a whole number, either in the form of a number of minutes or as a specific number of units to do (e.g., three calls), can make a task you are avoiding a lot easier to face. Always pick a number that feels comfortable, no matter how small. If you start feeling resistance when you choose your goal, scale back further.

You can also use whole numbers to limit activities that you tend to get lost in, or that you generally spend too much time doing. Be sure to set the timer far enough away that you have to get up to turn it off.

Exercises

Looking at your job-search action plan, choose some of the tasks that you can see yourself avoiding. Enter them in the table below, and decide how much you will do in one session for each task, either using task units (e.g., three new LinkedIn invitations), or a specific number of minutes.

Task	Whole-Number Goal

The following questions are designed to make you more aware of how you may be wasting time, and help you use whole-number goals to come up with a plan to use your time better.

Taking breaks:

1. Do you find that, after working intensely for a while, you need to take a break?

    ___ Yes   ___ No (*skip to "Limiting Activities"*)   ___ Occasionally

2. Which statement is most accurate for you?

    ___ I take a brief break, then get back to work. (*skip to "Limiting Activities"*)

    ___ I plan to take a brief break, but it always ends up being longer.

3. How many minutes would you consider to be an appropriate amount for a break?

    ___ 5 minutes   ___ 10 minutes   ___ 15 minutes   ___ 20+ minutes

Limiting Activities

In the first column below, name up to three activities that must be done but suck you in—email, LinkedIn, etc.

In the second column, map out a specific plan for limiting those activities when you find yourself wasting time with them.

Activity	How Will You Limit It?

Tasks That Take Too Long

In the first column below, name up to three tasks that you generally spend too much time completing.

In the second column, write the amount of time that you often spend on these tasks.

In the third column, write down an amount of time that would be more appropriate for each of these tasks.

Task	How much time do you usually spend doing it?	How much time would be appropriate to spend on it?

Next we'll talk about creating routines in your day. If you're going to take a break now, be sure to schedule your next session and mark it on the calendar.

Make It Part of an Existing Routine

When I work with job-seekers, I find one of their biggest obstacles to productivity is the lack of structure in their lives. Routines can build in that much-needed structure. A routine is something you do automatically without even thinking about it. It saves having to decide what to do next.

If you didn't have routines, you'd have to make the same decisions every morning: do I first take my shower or brush my teeth? Do I get dressed before or after breakfast? Using brainpower to make the same decisions over and over again is a waste of time and energy.

Create a job-search routine by incorporating it into or combining it with a routine that's already in place. You can add the job-search routine before, after, or in-between established routines. The important thing is to do them one right after the other and always in the same order.

Do It at the Same Time Every Day

Think of something you already do regularly at the same time each day. "Piggy-back" your job-search routine to the existing routine by always doing it either immediately before or after the existing routine.

Working on the job search first thing (or at least early) in the morning is one of the most effective ways to be productive. Starting something else first can derail the whole day. Hopefully you eat a healthy breakfast everyday, so that's an already-established routine. For example, if you are signed up for an online class, a new routine would be to spend some time on the class every day immediately after you get up from the breakfast table, maybe with your morning coffee.

If you felt resistant to starting on your class as you finished breakfast, start with a small amount and slowly increase the amount that you do in one sitting over time. The important thing is that every single time you finish breakfast, you go straight to the classwork. Even if you only do it for a few minutes, it's building a habit.

You can do the same thing every day, as suggested above. Alternatively, pick specific items to do on specific days, but still establish the "work on the job search right after breakfast" routine on those days. For example, after breakfast:

- Monday: Search job boards and apply for positions.
- Tuesday: Spend time on LinkedIn.
- Wednesday: Find at least one networking event to attend and schedule it.
- Thursday: Connect with friends, family members, or former work associates.
- Friday: Create a job-search plan for next week.

Or it could be something as simple as, "Work on my job search for a specific amount of time right after breakfast every weekday." Decide ahead of time what you will choose to do during that period and how much you will do.

Once the routine is established, you can gradually extend the amount of time that you devote to it. If there is a morning when you can't do the full amount, try to do at least some amount to keep the routine going.

You can pick any already-established routine; breakfast was just one example.

Do It Before, During, or After a Specific Activity

Routines don't have to be tied to something that you do at the same time every day. They can be tied to a specific action—something you do regularly—at different times throughout the day or week.

Are you a dog owner? If so, your pet needs to go out a couple of times a day. After each time you let the dog out or take him on a walk, reach out to one person on your networking contact list.

Do you enjoy drinking coffee or tea? After you put the water on to heat up, check out one job board.

Think of anything you do regularly, not necessarily at the same time every day, and decide what job-search task you will do right before, during, or afterwards.

Summary

Attaching a new routine to an existing routine can be a very effective way to add structure to a seemingly unstructured day. Find some time directly before, during, or after an already-established routine, and slip in a new job-searching routine. Start with a small amount and increase the amount slowly if you feel some resistance.

Exercise

Think about a job-search activity that you want to do on a regular basis, as a regular routine. Then, using the table below, decide how to incorporate it into an existing routine.

Down the road, when your first new routine is firmly established, come back and decide how you will incorporate a second one.

New Routine	Existing Routine	How often do you do the existing routine?	How will you add the new routine to the existing routine?
		___ Once a day ___ Several times a day ___ Weekly ___ As needed ___ Other: _____	___ Do it right before ___ Do it right after ___ Do it during
		___ Once a day ___ Several times a day ___ Weekly ___ As needed ___ Other: _____	___ Do it right before ___ Do it right after ___ Do it during
		___ Once a day ___ Several times a day ___ Weekly ___ As needed ___ Other: _____	___ Do it right before ___ Do it right after ___ Do it during

If you aren't continuing on now, have you scheduled your next session?

Start Small and Increase Slowly

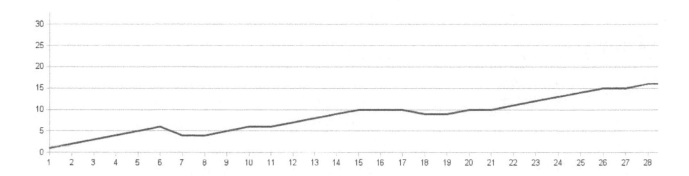

If you've been postponing your job search, or even just one aspect of it, it might be because you are feeling that you need to spend an intolerable amount of time on it each day. Or you might be feeling anxious or depressed. If any of these are true, you can become productive by giving yourself permission to start out doing just a little bit each day.

Prescription for Procrastination

Anytime you are stuck, the secret to getting started is starting small and building gradually:

- Pick one task and assign a small goal to it.
- Choose to do that amount regularly until you start to feel more comfortable with it.
- Then add a little to the goal.

You can set an amount—no matter how small—that you feel comfortable doing. This sets yourself up for success.

Tackling the Terrible

No matter how motivated you are, there are going to be job-search tasks that you just hate, hate, hate. Yet avoiding them might be really sabotaging your search.

When that happens, pick a very, very small whole-number goal to get started. Let's say you just despise writing cover letters. You have a line on a job that looks good, but you just can't seem to drag yourself to the computer to get going on it. Try setting the timer for a very small amount of time. Maybe 10 minutes, or just five minutes if 10 feels too daunting. Even two minutes will get you started.

Often people find that once they do a small amount on a task, they realize that it's not quite as bad as they expected. After your first tiny goal is reached, decide when you are going to do the next one. Maybe the next time you can up the amount a little bit. Or maybe do just the same amount again. No amount is too small if it gets you going. It's better to do five minutes a day than to do zero minutes because you thought you should do at least an hour.

When You Are Totally Stuck

If the job-search process is making you anxious and avoidant, you need to forgive yourself for not being as efficient and proactive as you "should" be. Accept that you might be feeling vulnerable, and that it's okay if you need to start by sticking your toe in the water. Don't beat yourself up for not jumping right into the deep end.

I'll talk about the importance of support later on in the book, especially if you are feeling down and demoralized. In the meantime, *any* progress—no matter how small—is forward motion and a step in the right direction. Baby steps are far better than no steps and, as you start to feel stronger, you can do more each day. Pick some very small and easy goals to work on, and start by doing just one or two in a day. For example:

- Call one person and tell them you are looking for employment. Pick someone you trust and who cares about you.
- Spend five minutes writing a description of your most recent job responsibilities.
- Find two job posting sites on the Internet and bookmark them in your browser.
- Search "career centers near me" and bookmark the results in your browser.

Even if you just do one of these each day, you are back on the trail. After a few days of doing just one, try increasing the amount or doing two items. Celebrate each accomplishment, no matter how small. Congratulate yourself for getting moving again! It will take a while to get up to speed, but focus on what you have done, not what you haven't done. That's easier to say than to do, but when you start feeling better about yourself you'll be less likely to stick your head in the sand (or in a computer game).

Summary

By starting small and increasing slowly when you feel stuck, you can stop avoiding and get going on what you need to do. Remember to assign the goal by what you are *willing* to do, not by what you think you *should* do. Pick an amount and notice how it feels—does it feel like you can tolerate doing that much? If not, pick a smaller number. If something feels so bad that even one minute is too much, then you probably need to do some deep thinking about what's really going on for you. I'll address that in the chapter *Overcoming Obstacles*.

Exercise

Think of 1–3 job-search tasks that you see yourself avoiding. For each one, fill out the table below. The first row is filled out as an example.

Task	Starting Whole-Number Goal	Amount of Increase	Frequency of Increase	Final Goal
Complete online JavaScript class	5 minutes, 5x per week	5 minutes	Each week	30 minutes a day

Feel free to update the table as you work on the task. You might find you were overly optimistic or pessimistic when you decided on your amounts and frequency of increase.

Are you going to start on the next chapter now? If not, when will you do it? Remember to schedule it on your calendar.

Reward Yourself

How can you motivate yourself to do a task you're avoiding but know is important? Consider giving yourself a reward when you finish it. There are different kinds of reward systems that can be highly effective and surprisingly simple to implement.

Premack's Principle

In the 1960s, David Premack, Ph.D., a psychologist at the University of Pennsylvania, formulated Premack's Principle: "More probable behaviors will reinforce less probable behaviors."[5] A "more probable behavior" is something that you do naturally, either because you must or because you enjoy it. A "less probable behavior" is something important you want to incorporate into your life, but you avoid because maybe you don't enjoy it or it doesn't come naturally. You can use the more probable behavior as a "carrot" for the less probable one. Your mom used Premack's Principle when she said you couldn't have dessert (the more probable behavior) unless you eat your vegetables (the less probable behavior).

Although very simple, Premack's Principle can be a powerful tool for working on your job-search activities. Think of the more probable behavior as your "reward." Pair a more probable behavior—which you know you'll do—with a less probable activity on your job-search action plan that you want or need to accomplish. The more probable behavior is something that you know you will reliably do (like eating lunch) or something you really enjoy (like reading a book).

Creating a Routine

If you want to create a routine, using Premack can be a powerful way to establish it. In this case you always do the less probable job-search routine directly before the more probable, already-established "carrot" routine.

Case Study: Dealing with Paperwork

In my own life, I use Premack's Principle to deal with the annoying pile of paper on my desk that accumulates each day. I know I will always read my email. That's the high-probability activity. But I don't allow myself to read email until I've spent 20 minutes in the morning working on the paper pile (or I get through the pile). It's now such a strong routine for me that the paperwork always gets done.

Case Study: Getting Dressed

Valerie found that once she went downstairs in the morning in her bathrobe, she tended to stay in her pajamas most of the day, which she didn't like doing. It felt like her day never really started. So we identified "going downstairs" as the high-probability activity and "getting dressed" as the low-probability activity. We came up with a plan where she could stay upstairs in the morning as long as she wanted, but she couldn't go downstairs until she was dressed. That worked perfectly for her. Using Premack's Principle can be that simple.

By the way, do you get dressed each weekday? Or do you find yourself lounging around in pajamas or sweatpants? You'll find you're much more productive if you get dressed first thing each morning. Like Valerie found out by staying in her pajamas all day, her day never felt like it really started. Save loungewear for weekends and holidays.

Bribing Yourself

You can also pick something you enjoy doing as a reward for working on your job search. It doesn't have to be something big or special, just something that you like and do regularly—such as reading a book or going onto social media. And you don't have to do the rewarding activity directly after the target activity you are trying to cultivate. It could be a delayed reward. For example, you could say, "I only get to watch TV tonight if I apply to three jobs this afternoon."

Case Study: Alternating Between Work and Breaks

When Beth has a task she's really struggling to stay focused on, she bribes herself with the help of her timer. She does 20–30 minutes of focused work, followed by 10–15 minutes of a computer activity she enjoys. She feels 20–30 minutes is manageable, and there's always a respite that's never far away.

A Word of Caution

Premack's Principle is powerful but also fragile, especially at first. Once you slip and allow yourself the more probable activity without doing the less probable one, the principle's effectiveness is pretty well compromised. Think carefully and realistically about how much you want to accomplish and the reward you're going to pair it up with.

Start with a small goal. Aim for consistency, withholding the reward for the behavioral change, and slowly increase the amount of the goal over time. Down the road, when the sequence is well-established, an occasional cheat won't derail you. But hang tough in the beginning.

Big Ticket Rewards

You can also reward yourself with something special that you wouldn't otherwise get around to giving yourself. Is there something that you've been wanting to do, like a day of hiking or coffee with a friend? Obviously you can't say, "Okay, I made two contacts this morning, now I get to go visit a friend for the weekend." Instead, you can earn your reward by using the equivalent of a sticker chart. We generally think of these as being only for children, but they can be very effective motivators for adults too.

Draw a grid on a piece of paper with a specific number of squares on it, maybe 25 or 50 or 100. The bigger the reward the more squares you'll want to do, but limit it to 100 tops. Each time you complete a mini-goal, put a check mark in one of the squares. It's a great visual way to chart your progress and when the squares are filled you've earned your reward. Each square could be a specific amount of time worked, a number of contacts made, applications filled out, or any other item from your job-search action plan.

Be sure to give yourself the reward when you've earned it. It's amazing how often people work hard for a reward and then don't give it to themselves—or up the ante!

Additional Motivation

For particularly difficult tasks or habits, you can double up the rewards. For example, don't allow yourself to watch TV in the evening unless you've finished one online class lesson during the day. And when you've completed ten lessons, allow yourself something special.

Summary

If you set them up correctly and follow through, rewards—from simple everyday activities to special events—can be powerful motivators for achieving goals. They don't have to be complicated or elaborate. You can base Premack's Principle on everyday behaviors, or on things you regularly enjoy doing as motivators. You can use a chart to earn a big ticket reward.

Exercises

In the table below, write down three high-probability activities that you reliably do on a regular basis, like eating lunch or going downstairs in the morning. Then write down a less-than-favorite job-search task that you can pair with each one of them. The pairings you create should have the same regularity. That is, pair low-probability things you want to do daily, with high-probability activities you already do daily. Pair weekly things with weekly things and so on.

High-probability Activity (Something you already do reliably on a regular basis)	Low-probability Activity (Job-search activity)

Now write down a few simple activities that you enjoy on a regular basis. Then write down the tasks or activities that you can use to earn these rewards. Again, pair things that have the same regularity.

High-probability Activity (Something you enjoy doing)	Low-probability Activity (Job-search activity)

Finally, write down some "big ticket" rewards, some activities you want to accomplish, and how you will use a chart to earn those special rewards.

"Big Ticket" Reward	Activity	Number of squares in chart	How much will you do to check off one box?

Now go back through the tables, look at the different ideas that you came up with, and decide which ones you want to implement. Write your plan down in the chart on the next page. Start with only one, maybe two, and wait until those become second nature before choosing another one to start.

Activity	Reward (Something you do reliably, or enjoy doing, or "big ticket")	Notes on how you will implement this plan

Don't forget to schedule your next session on your calendar if you are going to take a break now. Or maybe set your timer for a break and come back to the workbook when the timer goes off!

Make It a Commitment

When we plan to do something, we often say something like "I'm gonna try to..." The word "try" gives us an out and denotes a certain lack of seriousness about following through. Instead, make your plans *commitments*.

What is a commitment? Abraham Lincoln defined it perfectly when he said, "Commitment is what transforms a promise into reality. It is the words that speak boldly of your intentions. And the actions which speak louder than the words. It is making the time when there is none... Commitment is the stuff character is made of; the power to change the face of things."

When you agree to wed, you make a commitment to the marriage, even when the going gets rough. You don't say you'll "try to" take this person as a spouse. You say, "I DO."

Yet, when we plan to work on our job-search action plan, the level of sincerity we often have is, "I'll try—if it isn't too hard." How can we change our intentions into a real commitment?

Make a Public Declaration

Let people know what you are going to do and ask them to hold you accountable. Put yourself on the spot.

Your "public" declaration can be to a few people or a few hundred but, no matter what the number, tell people exactly what your plan is. Specifically:

- **What** action you are going to take,
- **When** you are going to have it completed, and
- **How they will know** that you did it.

Do It Despite Adversity

It's an amazing self-esteem boost when we find a way to forge ahead despite the fact that the going gets tough. It's easy to use adversity as an excuse for not following through. Finding a way around problems is the level of commitment that Lincoln was talking about. What if your life depended upon your following through? Act as though it does even if it doesn't. When you are really determined to push through, you can be amazingly creative. If you planned to work on cover letters first thing in the morning but your toilet overflows, work on them later in the day—even if it means doing them when you were planning to relax.

Are You Ready?

When you think you might be ready to commit to a job-search task you've been avoiding, make sure you have given it some serious thought. Like with any other commitment, don't make it impulsively, or during an emotional moment of guilt, regret, or even euphoria. We've all heard the saying, "Marry in haste, repent at leisure."

Before you commit, ask yourself over the period of a few days, "Am I really, really committed to making this happen?" And remember, you don't have to commit to completing the entire task, just to doing one step.

Summary

How serious are you about finding a job? On a scale of 1 to 10, with 10 being completely committed to the job search, what score would you give your commitment level? There's no right or wrong number, but do some soul searching. Being honest with yourself about how committed you are can help you know if you really want to find a job, or are mainly giving it lip service. If you can truly give yourself a 9 or 10, making a commitment to yourself, or to a supportive person or group, can help you push through your resistance.

Exercise

The questions on the next page can help you think through how serious you are about committing to a task. Note this is not an exercise to be completed now, but questions to guide you going forward as you plan each week.

Task:_____

1. Are you *really* ready to make a commitment to start working on it?

    ___ Yes   ___ No *(an honest answer, reschedule it on your master timetable and skip the rest of the questions)*

2. When do you commit to getting started on this task?

3. How much do you commit to doing?

4. To whom will you announce it?

5. How will you let them know you did it?

6. What are some of the things that could *legitimately* get in your way?

7. What's your contingency plan if something unexpected comes up?

In the next chapter, you'll start planning your upcoming week. This is a good time to work on it, while the strategies you just learned are fresh in your head. If you don't want to do it now, decide when you will come back to it and put it on your calendar.

Make Your Decisions Ahead of Time

Plan your days ahead of time, not as you go along. We humans are not always good at making the right decision in the moment. If we're feeling anxious, we'll search YouTube kittens instead of job boards. If we're tired, we'll check Facebook instead of filling out job applications. If we're feeling avoidant, we'll do low-priority activities instead of the ones we really need to be doing.

Planning Ahead

Now that you have created your master timetable, you will use it to plan each week. Otherwise you may end up doing whatever's in front of your nose (remember those "Urgent But Not Important" items on page 19?) instead of keeping on track with your job-search action plan.

On Fridays, or some other specified time during the weekend, look at your master timetable for the upcoming week and decide how you are going to plan getting the tasks done. Keep these things in mind as you plan your week:

- Break down any overwhelming or distasteful tasks into smaller pieces.
- Assign whole-number goals to each task.
- Start with small, non-intimidating goals if you are feeling anxious, depressed, or avoidant.
- Decide whether or not you are truly *committing* to doing the task.

When you are making a plan, be sure to make each of the activities "SMART" ones. That is, all of the activities in your plan should be:

Specific: What exactly are you planning to achieve? ("Find an MS Office class.")

Measurable: How much will you do? ("I'll spend 45 minutes looking.")

Action-oriented: What action are you going to take? ("Search Internet for online classes and look at local community college offerings.")

Realistic: Is it realistic for you? ("Is this something I can truly do?")

Timely: When are you going to do it? ("Right after lunch")

There are two ways you can create the plan. One is with a weekly/daily schedule and the other is with a to-do list.

Creating a Weekly/Daily Schedule

Referencing the tasks on next week's master timetable page, fill in the weekly planner at the end of this chapter. First list the items for each day that you will *commit* to doing. Those are the ones that you *will absolutely do* first each day. It might be helpful to number them in the order you will do them.

Be aware that activities almost always take at least twice as long as you think they will. Plan for that. My clients are usually amazed at how much longer it took to get something done than they expected. Even on a day when you have no appointments scheduled, only list under "Commitments" what you know you can truly complete in 2–3 hours. You might want to add a time to each item. It can be very specific like "10:00 a.m." or less specific like "Start before noon."

As you plan each item, write down:

- **What** you are going to do;

- **How much** you are going to do; and

- **When** you are going to do it.

Instead of using the weekly planner form, you can schedule your daily commitments on your calendar, just like an appointment. This has been shown to be a highly effective strategy for getting things done. In fact, studies show scheduling tasks improves your chances of following through by 70%.[6]

To make this work, remember that past behavior is an excellent predictor of future behavior—and a *much* better predictor than what you think you "oughta" do. If you are someone who settles right down to work in the morning, just having the daily list without specifying times will be good enough. If your days seem to fly by before you even get started on your list, schedule the items on your calendar and use a timer or set an alarm for the time you need to get started on each item.

Once the list of commitments (and their start times, if needed) for each day is complete, list the optional items that you will only do *after* the commitments are done. Those might include some personal tasks you need to get done. Hang tight to this scheme when each day comes. It will be really tempting to do the non-commitment items first, especially if the commitments are items you are avoiding. When I run a coaching group, it always amazes me how many people report that they got all of the optional items done, but few of the committed items. And they were the ones who chose what was a commitment and what was optional! It often takes a couple of meetings before they finally realize that the committed items *must* be done before they get to the optional items.

Make sure you schedule at least 1–2 days off each week. It's also good to leave some wiggle room in case something unexpected (like an interview!) comes up, or you over-plan. Also, be aware of obstacles, both real and imagined, that could throw a monkey wrench into the works. Life happens and monkey wrenches get thrown. What will you do to get back on track? Being aware of all of this can keep you from being blindsided when the unexpected happens.

Case Study: Getting the Job Search On Track

When I first started working with Tricia, she'd been unemployed for almost six months and still didn't have her résumé together. At the time, the economy was sluggish and she knew that finding a job was going to be an uphill battle. Tricia found herself wasting a fair amount of time on the computer looking at email, checking stock prices, and doing anything else she could think of to avoid the job search. Together, we started mapping out her days. First thing after breakfast, she would work on her résumé for 20 minutes, followed by 20 minutes (with the timer!) of looking at her email.

Midway through the morning, Tricia planned do some networking, reaching out to three contacts (note the use of a whole number) either by phone or email, then she'd spend 20 more minutes on her résumé. That made a pretty good morning for Tricia. We also planned out her afternoons, always with specific tasks at a specific time for a predetermined amount of time. After a week of this routine, Tricia had her résumé together and ready to send out.

We spent the remaining weeks of her job search making lists of people to call and company websites to watch, plus we included some personal projects that were in need of attention. Tricia's list always included the day and time she was going to do each item. Her efforts paid off. Despite the difficult economy, she found a new job within six months.

The To-Do List

Some people prefer to use to-do lists instead of mapping out their whole week. To-do lists are easy and convenient, but they have the problem that people tend to do the easiest or most enjoyable items first. The hardest and most disagreeable ones get put off until last. Then those "roll over" to the next list, and the next. Often they never get done.

Is your to-do list full of "rolling" items? It's a common problem, but one that can be managed by a strategy I've used for years.

I start by writing my to-do list on a piece of paper that has room for about 15 items. Some are five-minute items and some take longer. The list is comprised of both business items and personal ones. I make sure that each item includes a specific, measurable amount to do. If I need to work on my newsletter, I might put "20 minutes." If I need to record client hours for the week, I consider that as one task, as it only takes me a few minutes.

List #1 fills up as I think up things to do. When there's no more room on the paper, I start List #2 on a new piece of paper. **Now here's the really important part:** I make a *commitment* to myself not to start doing the items on the List #2, until *every single* item on the current list is done and crossed off. *No rolling items allowed!* This method gives me the freedom to complete the items on List #1 in any order, not necessarily in lock-step from top to bottom or on any particular day.

Sometimes when I think of a task that I don't want to do, I'll put it on List #2 instead List #1, even if there is still room on List #1. By writing it down, I've committed to getting it done but I've also given myself some time to work up the nerve to face it.

There are only two exceptions to my "Finish List #1 First" rule:

- An item on List #2 has a deadline that will expire before List #1 is complete. In that case, I complete that one List #2 item, then go back to List #1.

- An item on List #1 is completed as far as I can go. For example if I'm awaiting information or a reply from someone else, I'll cross it off List #1 and move it to List #2 so it doesn't slip through the cracks. It stays on my radar until it's completed. As long as I'm being honest with myself, I'm confident the item will get done in as timely a fashion as possible. Maybe I'll make a list item to remind the person who is the bottleneck to please get back to me.

Approaching my to-do lists this way has really helped with my own procrastination issues—I do have them! I know that once something is on a list it will absolutely get done. And yes, the most distasteful ones usually get done last. Knowing I need to get going on the stuff on List #2 forces me to finish up everything on List #1. Having personal and professional to-dos on each list is fine, as long as the personal items don't push the professional tasks aside. Once you complete the job-search stuff, getting a few personal items done can feel like a nice break.

Each list item answers the questions, "**What** am I going to do?" and "**How much** am I going to do?" The no-rolling-items rule answers the question, "**When** am I going to do it?" The implicit answer is, "Before I start on List #2." When List #1 is complete, List #2 becomes List #1 and you can start a new List #2.

When one of those "I should do this while I'm thinking about it" ideas comes to mind, I resist the urge and add it to my list instead. I always remember that once it's on a list it *has* to get done. That helps me decide if it's really important enough to be listed, or just something I am using to avoid something else.

If you want use the above to-do list method for your job search, start by putting all of your tasks for the week on a list as described above. You can fill up List #1, then put spillover items onto List #2. Or you can leave some space on List #1 in case you think of something—professional or personal—that you would like to add, and add the rest of the items to List #2. You can even make a List #3 if needed.

With very few exceptions, I strongly recommend that you keep your to-do list on a piece of paper, tacked up in a conspicuous place. The problem with keeping lists on your phone, tablet, or computer is that you have to seek them out. Out of sight, out of mind. I've had clients make excellent and detailed to-do lists on a computer, then never look at them until our next coaching session.

If, however, you already keep your to-do list electronically, *and looking at it regularly* is already a habit that works for you, go ahead and continue. But make sure you limit each list to 15–20 items.

Plan to Procrastinate?

There are people who really thrive on the adrenaline of deadlines. I have a friend who finds that her brain works at its peak when she waits until the last minute to do certain activities. Otherwise she has a hard time focusing and staying sharp. But she also carefully plans her schedule so that everything else is done by the time she sits down to do her "under pressure" tasks. She's one of the most productive people I know.

Consider the following. Which statements describe you most closely?

Column A	Column B
I feel sharp and focused when I have a tight deadline.	I feel overwhelmed and panicked when I have a tight deadline.
The work that I do when I'm under pressure is usually quite good.	The work that I do when I'm under pressure is thrown-together and substandard.
I feel really good after I produce a piece of work under pressure.	I feel bad about myself after I produce a piece of work under pressure.
I procrastinate because it seems to work for me.	I procrastinate because I'm avoiding something.

If you found that the statements in Column A fit you best, then procrastination is a technique that works for you. But if the statements in Column B describe you better, then planning ahead will be a more productive—and less stressful—strategy for completing your job-search action plan.

Summary

Would you go for a trip without having a plan or a map? Probably not—so don't wander through your week getting to things whenever you get to them. And don't make decisions at the last moment—or when you're tired, hungry, or under pressure. Instead, plan ahead and make your decisions ahead of time. Working from your master timetable to create either a to-do list or a weekly plan, decide exactly **what** you are going to do, **how much** you are going to do, and **when** you are going to do it. My regular reminders to put your sessions with this book in your calendar are examples of making your decision ahead of time.

It's Time to Plan Your Week

First, decide whether you think the to-do list or the weekly plan will work better for you. Then do one of them, as follows.

Create a To-do List

If the to-do list appeals to you, choose one of the following methods:

- A paper list (preferred)
- The notes on your phone (will you look at it regularly?)
- List on your computer (ditto!)

Using the tasks from your master timetable, create List #1 and (if needed) List #2. Leave some space at the bottom of each to fill in a few items you think of on the fly. Put items that are of lesser importance, or that you can't face quite yet, on List #2.

Create a Weekly Plan

Using the form on page 78,† create a plan for next week. Remember:

- The "Commitments" are the high-priority items that you *absolutely* will do first each day.
- The "Optional" items are the ones that you will not do until the day's commitments are completed—or done as far as possible.
- Items will almost always take longer to do than you expect.
- Build in wiggle room for when the unexpected happens. (It always does.)
- Ahead of time, think of possible obstacles that could get in the way. See page 79.
- Have a contingency plan in case the unexpected arises. (It will.)

---

† Copies are available on my website at *JSthatJS.com/Downloads*. Click on "Download Weekly Plan."

- Be sure to plan 1–2 days off from the job search each week.
- Optionally, schedule your commitments in your daily calendar and set an alarm to remind you when it's time to start.

One Final Note

When you pick an item to work on, concentrate only on that one thing. Don't try to second-guess yourself, wondering if you chose the "correct" item to do. You might want to choose an item by its priority, or choose an easier item to get you going on making progress.

If you are going to stop now, be sure to schedule your next workbook session!

Weekly Commitments

Week # _____ Dates _____ – _____

MONDAY		
What	**How Much**	**When**
Commitments (Do Or Die)		
Optional (If I Have Time)		

TUESDAY		
What	**How Much**	**When**
Commitments (Do Or Die)		
Optional (If I Have Time)		

WEDNESDAY		
What	**How Much**	**When**
Commitments (Do Or Die)		
Optional (If I Have Time)		

THURSDAY		
What	**How Much**	**When**
Commitments (Do Or Die)		
Optional (If I Have Time)		

FRIDAY		
What	**How Much**	**When**
Commitments (Do Or Die)		
Optional (If I Have Time)		

WEEKEND		
What	**How Much**	**When**
Commitments (Do Or Die)		
Optional (If I Have Time)		

What obstacles could you encounter?

What is your contingency plan to complete the commitment if something unexpected happens?

Get Support

For many of us, it takes the support of others to keep us on the straight and narrow, especially when the going gets tough. I often hear people tell me they think they "should" be able to achieve their goals on their own. But there's a reason support groups are so popular and effective: many people have a higher rate of success when they have others supporting them, encouraging them, and holding them accountable. Sometimes just hearing yourself tell your plans to someone else can  really solidify your ambitions. If you aren't proceeding well on your own with the employment search, reach out for help. It is not a sign of weakness. It's a sign of courage and commitment.

Check Out Local Career Centers

American Job Centers, also known as One-Stop Career Centers, or "One-Stops," are sponsored by the U.S. Department of Labor and provide a full range of services to those seeking employment. What's even better is that services in most One-Stops are free of charge. You can just call, walk in the door, or register online, depending upon the state and location.

Most areas of the country have One-Stops. Their locations are listed online at *www.careeronestop.org*, under the "Find Local Help" tab. Contact them to learn how to register for their programs. A more complete description of One-Stop Career Centers can be found in Appendix C of this book.

If you have a documented disability—whether physical, emotional, or cognitive—your local Vocational Rehabilitation Center can also be a valuable resource. While One-Stops often help people with various kinds of disabilities, Vocational Rehabilitation Centers are more specialized at finding jobs for people with disabilities. VRCs work with people looking for all levels of employment, from unskilled-labor jobs to professional jobs for people with advanced degrees. You can learn more about VRCs, including how to find one in your area, in Appendix D at the back of this book.

Some disability support groups, like the Epilepsy Foundation, also offer employment services for their target population.

Colleges, universities, and technical schools often provide career support to their alumni. If you graduated from a post-secondary institution, check out what resources they might be able to offer you.

Professional Recruiters

Recruitment specialists, also known in the vernacular as "headhunters," can be an excellent resource for job searchers looking for professional positions. External recruiters are paid by the hiring company, not by the job searcher. Job seekers and recruiters are on the same side—if you get a job, they get their fee. Internal recruiters work for the company that is looking to fill the job. Steer clear of recruiters who charge you a fee.

Use your network to find the names of good recruiters. Many specialize in specific industries, although there are recruitment companies that span a range of industries. Many local libraries have recruiter directories available. Oya's Directory of Recruiters, *i-recruit.com*, is an online resource that allows you to find recruiters by industry and location. Other free online guides include *onlinerecruitersdirectory.com*, and *searchfirm.com*. LinkedIn also has recruiters' profiles.

Who Are Your Support People?

Support can come from one person or from a group. Supporters can be others who are also hunting for a job, or just people who have their own goals that they also want support with. They need to be people you can turn to, who will help you through the rough parts, and who will keep you honest if you start to lose focus. You don't want to choose people who are overly harsh and critical. But on the other hand you also don't want a "poor baby" supporter who will accept your excuses and thereby unintentionally support your failure.

You need support people who will "hold your feet to the fire" when it would be too easy for you to cave in—people who will encourage and gently nudge you to see through your excuses.

When you tell your support person/people your intentions, make them very specific. Tell them:

- **What** actions you are going to take to further your job search.
- **How** much you are going to do on each item (use a whole number).
- **When** you are going to do them.
- **How they will know** that you did them.

Let them know you want them to hold you accountable, and will depend on them to do so. Tell them that if you do not follow through, they need to ask you why. And if your reason sounds like an excuse they need to call you on it.

You can also hire support people. Using professionals can be highly effective because they have special training to provide support, ideas, knowledge, and accountability. Career coaches, employment counselors, life coaches, and ADHD coaches are all examples of people who can effectively help you in your job search. They can function as cheerleaders, educators, and mirrors—reflecting back to you what they observe, helping you learn about yourself, and discovering the root of what is holding you back.

Join a Support Group or Create One of Your Own

Many employment centers run networking groups that meet regularly. Some have support groups that will help you set weekly goals, then report on how you did the next week. If you don't have access to an established support group, here's how to create one of your own.

The Who

Many local employment centers have a networking group. Attend the meetings and see if you can start a job seeker support group with people you meet at the networking meetings. Or create a group on *www.meetup.com*.

If you were laid off due to the shutdown of a company or division, you might reach out to your former co-workers to create a group. You will be able to offer each other positive support in a way others might not understand. Even if you don't create a formal support group with them, it's still good to keep in touch on a regular basis. They understand what you are going through and you can still share ideas and offer advice. When one of them finds a job, you want to be high on their list of people to remember when their company has an opening.

The When

Meet weekly and check in daily. The weekly meetings can be up to an hour long. A daily check-in call is very powerful and shouldn't take more than 10 minutes.

The Where and How

Weekly meetings can be in person, via conference call, or via Skype. Daily check-in calls should only be via conference call or Skype. There are many good, and free, conference call services out there. I personally use Free Conference Pro, *www.freeconferencepro.com*, but there are others you can find online. One person in your group can create an account, and will receive a bridge line phone number. They will create an access code to share with the other members. All of the group members call the bridge line at an appointed time, and calls can be recorded if a member can't attend.

The What

If possible, try to have the weekly calls at the beginning of the week. I suggest that each of you rotate leading the weekly and daily meetings. A weekly meeting agenda might look something like this:

- Round robin check-in with suggested ideas for sharing:
  - What they accomplished during the past week
  - Their successes
  - Status of the past week's commitments
  - What went well
  - What didn't go well
  - What they've learned this week
- Discussion topic
- Round robin, commitments for the next week
- Round robin, take-away from the meeting

Daily calls should take place early in the day and only include:

- What were yesterday's commitments?
- Which ones were accomplished?
- What will be done about the ones that weren't accomplished?
- What are the commitments for today?
- Any leads to share?

It's very important that the leader keeps the daily calls short and reminds people to be brief in their statements.

Members of the support group can reach out to people who have dealt with similar unemployment circumstances and have successfully found employment. Not only are they good networking connections, but they can give the group hope during those times when someone is feeling discouraged or the going gets rough. They might be willing to join the group on one of the weekly calls to share what worked for them in getting a job.

Working through this book together might serve as a base for the weekly topics.

Case Study: A Workplace Productivity Support Group

Here's an example from my own life to show how effective a support group can be. I was fortunate to work as a computer programmer at AT&T Bell Laboratories back when it was one of the research meccas of the world. My colleagues were among the best and brightest in their fields, and passionate about their work. Yet even these accomplished professionals found themselves struggling with time management and procrastination. A group of us decided to start meeting regularly to set goals. By mutual agreement, we were tough on ourselves. Goals were considered carved-in-stone commitments. If you didn't follow through on your commitment, you had to tell the group what you could (should!) have done differently to complete your goal. Our group's productivity increased immediately, as did overall job satisfaction. People were much happier when they knew they were regularly being held accountable.

A major perk of working in our division was infinite flextime. No one cared what hours you worked, as long as a high-quality job got done in a timely fashion. This was a blessing for some, but a curse for others. One member of our group, Cindy, cruised into work around 5 p.m. each evening and worked late into the night. Management didn't care; she did excellent work and always got things done. But Cindy herself wasn't happy about her chosen work hours. The problem was that she would get distracted when at home, spending time on whatever came into her field of vision. By not having set work hours, she wasted her day at home doing trivial things she didn't really care about. So Cindy made a commitment to our group, that she was going to be at work at 9:00 a.m. sharp every day. She wasn't going to get there at 9:05 or even 9:01; she would be in her chair by 9:00 a.m. on the dot. We were strict! I'll never forget the day I looked out my window to see her bolting across the parking lot to make it on time. She did it, and was very pleased with her new schedule.

We used our group to set personal goals as well, and Cindy made several commitments just before we took off for the Christmas holidays. I received an excited phone call from her during that time. "I can't believe it!" she said. "I can't believe how much energy I have because of this group! It's wonderful. I'm so happy!" Being part of our tough-love little group really did change Cindy's life.

Never underestimate the importance and effectiveness of good support. If you're in such a group, make sure the members understand that the power of the whole group lies in following through on commitments. When one person doesn't follow through it weakens the group and gives everyone an "out." Our support group at Bell Labs worked so well because we agreed that we were serious about accountability.

Hiring a Coach

Career coaches will help you figure out what kinds of jobs are most appropriate for your skill set, or support you in transitioning to a new career. They will help you in making informed decisions about your goals, as well as assist you in finding the right tools to meet those goals. They know the ways to make you stand out in a sea of applicants, and know how to uncover openings that aren't online. Some with clinical experience can also help you understand how you might be getting in your own way, and provide support with the anxieties and fears that can go along with a job search. They won't find a job for you, but they will equip you with the tools to make your search more effective and efficient.

Life coaches are trained specifically to help you find the obstacles that are keeping you stuck. They help you examine the beliefs, mindsets, and habits that might be getting in your way. They have no agenda other than to assist you towards reaching your goals, and can be more objective than a close friend or family member can often be. Most people find working with a coach to be very effective for achieving goals.

If you have ADHD, or suspect that you may, working with a life coach or career coach who has specific ADHD training is crucial. An ADHD-trained career coach will assist you in figuring out what kinds of careers are most appropriate for someone with your specific ADHD challenges. There are many different ways that ADHD presents itself, and a career path that works for one person with ADHD may be a disaster for another.

Many people with diagnosed or suspected ADHD suffer from shame and poor self-esteem because they've often been criticized by teachers, parents, bosses, and others who don't understand the impact of having ADHD. All of this can work against the job search, as the confidence of those with ADHD is already undermined. Bad feelings can be further reinforced, as the person with ADHD struggles to stay on track with the job search. ADHD coaches will help you find individualized strategies for the job search, uniquely tailored to your style of approaching tasks. They can provide additional insights and help you work with—not against—who you are. The skills learned from an ADHD coach will also help you once you're back in the workforce.

Before you hire any career coach, life coach, or ADHD coach, make sure he or she has been certified by a reputable professional certification organization. Certification indicates that the coach is appropriately trained and has demonstrated a specific level of proficiency defined by the credentialing organization.

If you're considering hiring a life coach, interview several coaches that have been certified by the International Coach Federation (ICF) or the Center for Credentialing & Education (CCE). The

ICF website, *www.coachfederation.org*, and the CCE website, *www.cce-global.org*, both have listings of certified coaches. The ICF website also has suggestions for questions to ask when interviewing a potential coach.

ADHD coaches should be certified by organizations such as the Professional Association of ADHD Coaches (PAAC), *http://paaccoaches.org*, or by one of the coaching schools listed on its website (currently ADD Coach Academy, *www.addca.com;* and MentorCoach, *www.mentorcoach.com*).

You needn't be constrained by geography. Most life coaches and ADHD coaches meet with their clients by phone, and some meet in person as well. In my practice, I work with most of my clients by phone, some hundreds or thousands of miles distant. I find people who are already struggling with managing their time don't need the overhead of extra travel. But that doesn't work for all clients. If you feel you need to work with someone in person, search the websites suggested above for local coaches who work in person.

Career coaches can be found at your local career center or employment services program. You can also hire a private career coach, but check their credentials and experience before you do. Look over their website, and research them on LinkedIn. Request references as well. Ask how many sessions most of their clients require. And don't expect instant results in just one or two meetings. It takes time for a good career coach to really understand you and get you on your way.

After you've interviewed a few potential coaches, choose the one that feels like the best fit. Trust your gut.

Case Study: Getting Out of the Gate

Anthony, a single guy in his 40s, left a job he hated, figuring he could live on his savings for a few months while he looked for a new position. But six months went by, and he hadn't even started his search. He contacted me after attending a presentation I gave at a One-Stop Career Center. We only worked together for 4 sessions, because that's all the time it took to get him up and running. Making a plan with me each week, having the accountability of knowing I would check his progress the following week, and talking over deeper stumbling blocks, was all it took to get him on track. A big reason he progressed so quickly was that before each session he was very diligent about filling out my weekly focus form, which consists of 5 questions:

1. What are you grateful for this week?
2. What have you accomplished since our last session?
3. What are you learning about yourself?
4. What do you want to talk about during this week's session?
5. What do you want to have in place at the end of this week's coaching session?

Many coaches use a similar focus form, making the coaching sessions efficient and on point. Like most coaching clients, Anthony found that not only did he accomplish a significant amount, he also learned a lot about himself.

Summary

No matter where you find support—be it a group, a friend, or a professional—don't be shy about reaching out to others when you're looking for a job. It can make the difference between making forward progress and being stuck for weeks, months, or even years.

If you haven't done so already, look up "One-Stop Career Centers" on the Internet and find one near you. If you are challenged with any disability—ADHD, Asperger's syndrome, or any other disability for which you have a diagnosis—check out your local Vocational Rehabilitation Center.

If you can't find a job-search support group in your area, form one on your own. Always choose people who will give you tough love in a caring way. Support is critical, but critical people are not supportive. *Shaming and verbal abuse are not helpful!*

A private career coach, life coach, or ADHD coach can be well worth the money spent if that's what it takes to get you back to earning a salary more quickly. Some coaches do group work, which may be less expensive, and group members can learn a lot from each other.

No matter which route you choose, if you get stuck, don't try to go it alone. Reaching out can be hard but I've never worked with a client or a group that wasn't glad they made the connection.

Exercises

Take some time to think about getting support, and find resources in your area that can help you if you get stuck. Even if you don't need them right now, these will be good to have on hand if you become stuck later.

If you were to reach out for support, what kind of support do you think would be the most helpful? Place a check mark next to each resource you think you might use:

____ A local One-Stop Career Center or Vocational Rehabilitation Center

____ Your college career center (if they provide services to alumni)

____ A private professional career, life, or ADHD coach

____ An established support group

____ A support group that you create to meet regularly

____ A casual group of fellow job seekers

____ One or two (or more) close friends or relatives to help keep you on track

____ Other: _____

For each item you chose above, fill out the following, as appropriate:

A local One-Stop Career Center or Vocational Rehabilitation Center: Find out what ones are located in your area. Check their websites to learn about programs and services they offer. List their locations and contact information:

Your college career center: Check to see what services they offer alumni. If you received degrees from more than one institution, check them all. Write down the contact information and service provided for each one:

A private professional career, life, or ADHD coach: Spend some time on the Internet looking for coaches who seem to be a good match for you. Also, ask acquaintances if they know any career, life, or ADHD coaches they could recommend. Write the names and contact information of several coaches you might like to interview or would consider working with:

An established support group: Research to find some support groups for job hunters. Possible resources include your local paper, *www.meetup.com*, or local career centers. Also search the Internet for job-search groups run by career, life, and ADHD coaches. Some life and ADHD coaches conduct mixed support groups for anyone looking to achieve any goal, not just job seekers. Although not appropriate for people who need specific career advice, they can provide a significant level of support for your job search at a reasonable price. Write down what you find here:

A support group to meet regularly that you create: What are some of the ways that you could meet fellow job seekers?

Are there people you already know through various networking groups that might be interested in forming a jobs-related group with you? If so, write down their names:

Fellow job seekers: Who do you currently know that is also searching for a job? Would they be willing to have you check in with them on a regular basis?

Friends: To whom could you reach out to for support on your job search?

Other: List here any other people you can think of who could support you in your search.

Part Five:

Wrapping It Up

Putting It All Together

By this point in our journey together, you have created your job-search action plan, created a master timetable, and learned strategies for getting and staying on track. In this chapter, you're going to create a plan of attack for any important tasks that you know you need to do but may have trouble getting motivated to complete. You might want to look back at your thoughts on Quadrant II (important but not urgent) on page 18 or take a look at your job-search action plan on page 35. You'll have a chance to go back and review the applicable exercises, and bring everything you found useful into one place for each obstinate goal. Not all of the tools will work for all of your goals all of the time, so don't try to force the issue if a tool doesn't seem to fit. There's no "one size fits all" here. It's about what works for you, now.

Start out by writing down the three tasks in your job-search action plan that, for whatever reason, you are most reluctant to do.

Egregious Task #1: _____

Egregious Task #2: _____

Egregious Task #3: _____

Now for each task, fill out the worksheets on the next pages.

Egregious Task #1: _____

Which of the tools will you use to complete this task?

✔	Tool	Page	✔	Tool	Page
	Avoid Your Personal Black Holes	26		Start Small and Increase Slowly	61
	Deal with Distractions	31		Reward Yourself	65
	Set a Whole-Number Goal	53		Make It a Commitment	70
	Make It Part of an Existing Routine	58		Get Support	88

Go back to the earlier chapters, and review the exercises you completed for each tool you checked off. Using everything you wrote in each exercise, create a strategy for tackling the task and write it down, or type it up on your computer.

Strategy for Completing Task #1_____
(name of task)

_____

_____

_____

_____

_____

_____

_____

_____

_____

_____

_____

_____

_____

Egregious Task #2: _____

Which of the tools will you use to complete this task?

✔	Tool	Page	✔	Tool	Page
	Avoid Your Personal Black Holes	26		Start Small and Increase Slowly	61
	Deal with Distractions	31		Reward Yourself	65
	Set a Whole-Number Goal	53		Make It a Commitment	70
	Make It Part of an Existing Routine	58		Get Support	88

Again, go back to the earlier chapters and review the exercises you completed for each tool you checked off. Using everything you wrote in each exercise, create a strategy for tackling the task and write it down, or type it up on your computer.

Strategy for Completing Task #2_____
(name of task)

_____

_____

_____

_____

_____

_____

_____

_____

_____

_____

_____

_____

Egregious Task #3: _____

Which of the tools will you use to complete this task?

✔	Tool	Page	✔	Tool	Page
	Avoid Your Personal Black Holes	26		Start Small and Increase Slowly	61
	Deal with Distractions	31		Reward Yourself	65
	Set a Whole-Number Goal	53		Make It a Commitment	70
	Make It Part of an Existing Routine	58		Get Support	88

Once more, go back to the earlier chapters and review the exercises you completed for each tool you checked off. Using everything you wrote in each exercise, create a strategy for tackling the task and write it down, or type it up on your computer.

Strategy for Completing Task #3_____
(name of task)

_____

_____

_____

_____

_____

_____

_____

_____

_____

_____

_____

_____

_____

_____

_____

_____

_____

_____

_____

_____

_____

_____

_____

_____

_____

Using this approach, you can now come up with plans for any task that you find yourself avoiding.

But What If…

Now you have your plans in place and are ready to move forward. For some people, that's all they need: a structure, an actionable strategy, and some tools to make it all work. But what happens if (or when) you start to slack off? And what if you're still having trouble starting even after you have a strategy? Sometimes you have to look deeper. Staying on track and exploring obstacles are the subjects of the next two chapters of this book.

There are no more exercises, except you might want to fill out the questionnaires in Appendix A if you haven't already. The rest of the book reads quickly so continue it now if you can. Otherwise, be sure to schedule your next—and probably last—session.

Staying on Course

What happens when the search runs into overtime and you start to lose steam? Maintaining forward momentum is hard. The initial adrenaline is wearing off, and discouragement may be setting in. These feelings are common and understandable but they don't have to be a deal breaker for your job search. Here are some coping mechanisms that might help.

The Importance of Self-Care

Are you taking care of yourself? How's your sleep? Exercise? Eating habits? Are you taking time out for the three R's—rest, relaxation, and recreation? When you're in the throes of a job search, it's not the time to slack off with self care. That'll just make things worse, physically and mentally. If anything, it's time to take better care of yourself. Your long-term self will thank you. Take a look at the wellness questions on page 125. Use those to help you think about the ways you can keep your spirits and energy up during the job-search process.

Decrease the Intensity

When keeping the pace becomes a struggle, it can be helpful to scale back for a while and then slowly increase job-search activities again. But don't stop completely; it's important to keep a routine going. Decide how much you can actually do today, even if it's only 10 minutes. When you are ready, start building back up slowly. Even when you don't do a lot, you're at least keeping some momentum.

Is Your Pace Maintainable?

Did you go from 0 to 100 mph when you started your job search? Do you think you should be working around the clock to find a job? Do you give yourself credit for each bit of progress, no matter how small, or do you berate yourself for not doing more in a shorter time? Have you chosen strategies in this book that just don't work for you? For example, some people work really well by breaking up a task into chunks as described in the chapter, *Break Your Tasks Down into Manageable Pieces*. Others like to plow through from beginning to end. The tools in this book are suggestions, not mandates. If pushing through to completion in a single sitting is your preferred style, by all means go for it!

Get Support

Gentle and positive support is critical when you start to slip. Harsh, critical support is counterproductive. People who shame you or make you feel guilty are not supportive; you're

102

already feeling bad enough yourself! The best support people help you find solutions, offer suggestions to optimize your time, and cheer you on in your job search.

Forgive Yourself

Just as harshly critical people aren't helpful, harsh self-criticism isn't helpful either. Has beating yourself up over something *ever* helped you improve? If that worked, we'd all be perfect. Beating on yourself, "should-ing" on yourself, or telling yourself "I just need to do it" are not effective. I've never known anyone to change through self-punishment. Sometimes people think that if they are hard enough on themselves, they will learn their lesson and do better. If you treated a child the way some people treat themselves it would be considered abusive. The child's self-esteem would plummet. But we freely, sometimes even gleefully, abuse ourselves.

What really works is determining the real obstruction. More about that in the next chapter. In the meantime, remember that self-flagellation takes important emotional energy away from the problem at hand and doesn't solve anything. Be careful what you say to yourself. Remember— you're listening!

Is Your Environment a Disaster?

If the place where you do your job searching is a disorganized mess, it's going to be hard to be effective and efficient. You might want to take some time right now to get on top of the chaos. Completing the questionnaire on page 117 *(Your Stuff and Your Space)* can help you get an idea of problem areas. If you need a easy-to-implement strategy to tame the clutter monster, Appendix B *(Getting Control of Your Environment)* has an approach that is simple and effective for getting a handle on the problem in record time. Don't make this an excuse to start organizing your environment while forgetting about the job search. First things first. But if your job-search space is holding you back, spend a little clean-up time to get it in order.

Join Toastmasters

Toastmasters International is a non-profit organization that helps its members improve public speaking, communication, and leadership skills. The skills gained through Toastmasters can help any job seeker, from service worker to professional. This is a great way both to network and develop self-confidence. You will learn how to think on your feet, or hone that ability even if you are already good at it. It's a highly important skill for job interviews and directly transferable to almost every job. Meetings are run by the members of each chapter to keep membership cost low.

Good communication skills are valued in every job. The ability to react and interact quickly and well with customers, peers, bosses, and subordinates is critical. The more resources you bring to any job, even an entry-level position, the more valuable and promotable you will become.

If you think Toastmasters could be helpful to you but find yourself avoiding it, take the first step (break it down or start small) by looking up Toastmasters on the Internet at *www.toastmasters. org*. See if there is a chapter near you. Ask a friend to go with you if you're uncomfortable going alone (get support).

Take a Deeper Look

Instead of just feeling bad about slip-ups or delays in the job search, do a little analysis. Drop the "shoulds," as in, "I *should* be able to do this!" (I hear that a lot as an ADHD coach.) Find out who you are and make changes that work *with* your style, not against your very nature. Try to figure out the "why" and the "what" of the blockages in your path.

Call In the Pros

If you find you just can't seem to stay on task on your own, it might be time to call in a professional. This is where coaching can be very helpful. It's the job of a coach to help you ferret out where you went off the track, and then work with you to come up with a reasonable plan.

Career coaches will help you figure out the *what* of the job search. They can help you decide what careers are best given your training, experience, and interest. They can critique your résumé so that it showcases your relevant abilities and background. If you are struggling with interview skills, they can practice with you to teach you how to present yourself in your best light. Career coaches know where to look to find the job openings, and how you can make yourself stand out among the competition.

Life coaches and ADHD coaches will help you with the *how* of the job search—as in how to stop procrastinating, how to set up a search plan, and how to stay on task. If you feel you can't afford to work with a life coach, find an accredited coaching school on the International Coach Federation website and contact them. Coaching schools sometimes have students who are willing to work with clients at a reduced rate.

But what if you can't even get to the maintenance stage—in fact, what if you can't even get started? Then it's time to take a deeper look at what's getting in your way. We'll look at possible obstacles in the next chapter.

Overcoming Obstacles

What happens when systems, plans, strategies, and structures aren't enough? You've worked your way through this book. You've done the exercises. You have a strategy. But somehow, you just can't get out of the gate. What then?

Sometimes when an approach isn't working, it just needs a little tweaking. You've probably already done that. But if you've tweaked it several times and still nothing is getting accomplished, it's time to look deeper.

"We can't solve problems by using the same kind of thinking we used when we created them."[†] Inappropriate or outdated belief systems can get in our way. There might be emotions that you need to understand before going forward. There are lots of reasons people get stuck. Here are some, along with suggestions for working through them.

Looking for the Wrong Job?

Do you really want the job or career you think you do? It's not always obvious. If you are looking for a job you dislike because you think that's what you went to school for, or because that's all you know, you might be erecting barriers without even realizing it.

Try accessing the services of your local career center, or a private career coach. They can give you assessments to find out where your skills, interests, and aptitudes lie. If you have any type of disability—physical, emotional, or intellectual—your local Vocational Rehabilitation Center may be the best resource. They work with people on all kinds of career paths, including skilled and unskilled labor, blue collar, and white collar jobs.

Going About It the Wrong Way?

If someone told you that there is only one way to do something, they have done you a grave disservice. Even if their idea worked perfectly for them, it may not work for you. That's not your failing, or the failure of their suggestion. It's just a bad match.

Respect that you might approach things in a different way. Do you prefer thinking with pencil and paper instead of typing on the computer? Then that's the best way to start working on your cover letter, your résumé, or even your job-search action plan.

---

† Attributed to Albert Einstein.

To-do list apps can be helpful, but only if they're convenient for you. If you have to work too hard to use one, it's not a good fit.

Networking is hugely important for job searching. There are many ways to network. If you'd rather spend the evening slamming your hand in a door than going to a large networking event, then find a different way. Don't waste time and energy deciding you "should" to go an event, register for it, then end up skipping it and berating yourself for days. Get creative and find other ways to network—perhaps through volunteering, friends and family, community activities, online, or other ways that you find more appealing and won't avoid.

Yes, you do have to step out of your comfort zone to find a job. But be realistic! Assign each strategy a number from 1–3, where 1 = "Easy-peasy, totally in my comfort zone," 2 = "Tough, but I can do it," and 3 = "I'd rather have open heart surgery without anesthesia." Forget the "shoulds." Use your time and energy in activities that are in the 1 and 2 category. Realistically you are not going to do the 3's so don't waste your valuable time or energy—even if your best friend touted them highly as can't-miss employment strategies.

Boundary Issues

Warren Buffett once said, "The difference between successful people and really successful people is that really successful people say no to almost everything."

It's common for clients to tell me they can't get to their own plans because other people keep asking them to do things. They can't say no. Sometimes it's a case of the "disease to please" and sometimes it's because they don't have the language or the skills to say no. Some people have been raised with the notion that saying no is selfish. Others find they enjoy being a "rescuer"—it makes them feel good, but at a cost to their productivity and the job search.

If you find it hard to say no, I highly recommend the book, *When I Say No, I Feel Guilty*[7] by Manuel Smith, PhD. Perennial wisdom for over 30 years, its message remains useful and relevant today.

Facing the Feelings

Sometimes the biggest obstacle to working on your job search is facing the feelings that come up as you begin to execute your plan. They can be lying just below the surface and you don't even realize they're there. But you subconsciously avoid working on your goal because, on some level, you know those feelings will surface when you get started. Shame, anxiety, anger, and sadness are just a few of the feelings that can keep us stuck, and we might not even realize we have them. Sometimes we look at jobs we think we "should" take instead of the ones that fit us the best. Then we wonder why we aren't motivated to move forward.

I had a client who was looking for a job, and she felt she should apply for a certain job posted in her town. For some reason, she just couldn't get moving despite knowing the application deadline was approaching. We looked carefully at different aspects of the job, and listed the associated pros and cons. I asked her to imagine herself actually holding the job and it was then that she realized she didn't want it. We conducted the same exercise with several other open positions, and in this manner she was able to figure out which jobs would be a better fit for her interests, abilities, and experience. She subsequently applied for several of them.

If emotions are getting in the way of your progress, writing about them (sometimes called "narrative therapy") is one way to uncover and face them. Talking to a trusted friend, clergy member, psychotherapist, or life coach can also help you figure out sticking points. Career coaches with clinical training as counselors can be helpful getting at even deeper issues.

Perceived Barriers: Advice from a Pro

Deborah Barnes, M.Ed, has been on both sides of the job search. She is currently a Workshop Facilitator and Certified Professional Résumé Writer at the North Shore Career Center in Salem, MA. Many years ago, she found herself looking for a job. One of the best pieces of advice she received during that period was to read a classic in its field, the book *Creative Visualization*[8], by Shakti Gawain. Now she recommends it to her clients. When asked why she found it so helpful, she says it taught her the following:

> What you focus on expands.
>
> You can focus on your perceived barriers—whatever they may be—or you can focus on what you bring to the table—your unique differentiators. Since body language is such a significant part of what we communicate, it will be clear to hiring managers what you are focusing on.
>
> You can spend your energy being a "Yeah, but…" person (we all know them; they are the people who have a reason that whatever you are suggesting isn't going to work) or a "Yes, and…" person. As with improvisational theater, you take what you're handed and go with it.
>
> Might that negative energy be better spent as positive energy—working on your résumé, interviewing techniques, and networking contacts—rather than getting together for a "pity party" with friends or former colleagues? In other words, don't water the weeds. Avoid negative people.
>
> In your job search—and your life—attitude determines whether it is an adventure or an ordeal. It is *your* choice.

What are *you* focusing on? Which do you choose, the adventure or the ordeal?

Acquiring Stuff

When I give a presentation, I say to my audience, "Raise your hand if you need more stuff." This is always met with chuckles and knowing nods of the head, as people think about how much stuff they already own. Most of us have just too darn much of it. It gets in our way, and it slows us down when we're looking for something, or doing anything. We have to dust it, store it, organize it, and move it out of the way. It's a huge impediment to getting things done.

When you go to a job fair or other career-related event, do you grab all the handouts and freebies? You probably figure, "I don't have time to look at this stuff now but I'll check it out when I get home." Do you actually check it out? Or does it just make the pile on your desk grow bigger? If you're already struggling with clutter and disorganization, chances are the stuff you take home will just make matters worse.

Besides degrading the quality of our lives, our overabundance of stuff is killing the planet. It takes energy and resources to manufacture and ship everything, and most of it ends up in a landfill or an incinerator without ever having fulfilled its intended mission.

Stuff costs us in many ways—money, time, energy, angst. It's taking over our houses, our offices, our desks, and our lives. If you have it, you have to manage it. You have to find a place to keep it or else it gets in your way. If it's out on the counter where it doesn't belong, it has to be put back. Unfortunately, all too often the place it "belongs" is on the top of a counter or piece of furniture, because it doesn't really have a home.

At the end of its useful life (if there ever was a useful life) we have to decide if we want to keep it or get rid of it. It all gets quite exhausting.

I've found the best way to deal with stuff is not to acquire it in the first place. That's easier said than done. We're hunter-gatherers by nature; it's fun to acquire stuff! But if it doesn't come into your life you don't have to worry about it. Really, how much of the stuff we own is useful or brings us pleasure? How do we keep the rest of it out of our lives?

The next time you are someplace where free stuff is staring you in the face, ask yourself the following questions before you reach out to take it:

- Where will I keep this once I get it home?
- When and how often will I actually use it?
- Where will it be in a week? a month? a year?
- What will ultimately happen to it?

If you end up never even looking at it—which happens all too often—it will end up cluttering your house until you eventually toss it. It's far easier to walk away without it than to have to deal with it in your space.

Think it over. If it isn't likely to enhance your life, don't take it.

Parting Thoughts

The only way I get anything done in life is by using the tools I have laid out in this book. They work. I use every one of them in both my personal and professional life.

I've really enjoyed writing this book, but that doesn't mean I'm always disciplined about working on it. I've used a lot of the tools to make it to the end, adapting them to suit my needs for this particular task. Here are the ones I used the most and how I used them:

Break It Down into Manageable Pieces: I'm a linear thinker and that's how I write. So I used the timer to chunk the amount of time I spent writing.

Set a Whole-Number Goal: I pretty much wrote this entire book in 20-minute chunks. Even on the days when I wrote for several hours overall, it was always with the timer going. In addition, I kept a pile of pennies and nickels on my desk. Each time the timer went off, I moved a penny to an "earned" pile. When I had earned five pennies, I traded them in for a nickel. Keeping score works for me!

Reward Yourself: I used my nickels to reward myself with an episode of a favorite TV show. One nickel (100 minutes of writing) = one episode.

Avoid Your Personal Black Holes: Once I start watching TV, I can easily slide into binge-watching. That's okay occasionally but not when it becomes a black hole. I can be very inertial once I get going, and it can be really hard to extract myself until I reach the end of the TV series—even if the series is several seasons long. Strict adherence to my reward system made me feel like I had earned the right to relax and even binge-watch occasionally. I'd save up my nickels for a weekend day when I just needed to "veg out." When the nickels were done, I stopped watching—honest!

Make It a Commitment: I reinforced my reward plan by texting it to my friend Martha. I reported back to her on a regular basis, and if I didn't, she'd proactively check in with me. That kept me on the straight and narrow.

I'm telling you about how I myself used the tools, because I want to encourage you to use them as you see fit. Adapt them to fit your style. You may want to use them exactly as presented to start with, but don't become a slave to the written word. Don't let them become another obligation, burden, or something else to feel bad about. They are tools, not rules. If they don't enhance your life, then don't use them. This book is about you and what you need to do to complete a successful job search.

My hope is that this book gives you new resolve and motivation for your job search. Maybe you already knew some of these things, or made up some similar tools of your own. If so, this book might be validating, and give you ways to expand on what you already do. Once you're employed again, the skills you've learned for staying on task in your job search will make you a more effective, more efficient employee. They can also help you manage your personal life.

Now go get 'em!

Part Six:

Appendices

Appendix A:
Looking at Your Life

The questionnaires in this appendix were originally created for my coaching practice, to help me gain a better understanding of my clients and their challenges. However, my clients often report that filling them out is a useful and thought-provoking exercise for themselves as well.

The questionnaires are about various areas of your life that may be affecting your job search. Responding thoughtfully to the questions in each section can give you additional insight as to why you may be struggling with the job search. Don't be intimidated by the number of pages. The questions are mostly multiple choice, so it shouldn't take you a long time to complete them. Some of them may be extremely helpful to you, others not so much. Use them as you see fit: modify the questions if necessary, and add your own if want. Check all that apply, pick the closest answers, or modify/invent answers if the provided choices don't work for you. The questionnaires address the job search, time, stuff, space, and information management.

There's no score to be tallied; there are no right or wrong answers. You don't "pass" or "fail." This is an exercise in self-awareness. The goal here is to give you an overall view of some areas of life management that can impact your job search. It's up to you to decide whether what you are doing works for you.

How You Spend Your Time

The way you use your time can significantly impact your job search, positively or negatively. It's important to achieve a good balance between personal time and job search time. Use the following questions as an awareness exercise for how your days are being spent, and what aspects of your life might be taking important energy and focus away from the job search.

Your Personal Time

I usually watch television (focused watching, not just having it on in the background):

___ Rarely.

___ Less than an hour per day.

___ Between 1 and 2 hours per day.

___ Between 2 and 3 hours per day.

___ More than 3 hours per day.

I waste time on the computer:

___ Rarely.
___ Less than an hour per day.
___ Between 1 and 2 hours per day.
___ Between 2 and 3 hours per day.
___ More than 3 hours per day.

When it comes to cell phone use, on a scale of 1–10 where

1 = "I generally use my cell phone only for emergency and essential phone calls," and
10 = "I tend to text or talk on my cell every free minute I have,"

I would give myself a rating of: _____.

The state of the overall organization of my house:

___ Is not a problem.
___ Makes accomplishing things take longer than it should.
___ Really causes me to waste a lot of time.

When asked to do something optional that I don't want or have time to do, I:

___ Almost always say no.
___ Usually say no.
___ Sometimes say no.
___ Usually say yes.
___ Almost always say yes.

My volunteer activities are:

___ Mostly things I enjoy and have time to do.
___ Obligations that I need to fulfill and have the time to do.
___ Obligations that I need to fulfill but don't have the time to do.
___ Opportunities to increase my skill set and my network.
___ Things I don't have time for and don't have obligations to fulfill, but I can't say no.

When it comes to downtime, on a scale of 1–10 where

1 = "My brain gets regular downtime," and
10 = "My brain is plugged into something every waking minute,"

I would give myself a rating of: _____.

I take time for leisure activities:

___ At least once a week.
___ A couple of times a month.
___ Rarely.
___ Yeah, right, who has time for fun?

Regarding recreation, on a scale of 1–10 where

1 = "I regularly take time for recreating (read: 're-creating')," and
10 = "I never take time to relax or have fun,"

I would give myself a rating of: _____.

Overall, on a scale of 1–10 where

1 = "My time is pretty calm and in control," and
10 = "My time is hopelessly frenetic,"

I would give myself a rating of: _____.

Your Stuff and Your Space

The state of your environment can significantly impact your efficiency as a job searcher. If your living space is a disaster, your disorganization will slow you down. As you go through this set of questions, think about whether your stuff and spaces are generally organized, or if they are so cluttered that it's causing you to spend valuable time looking for things.

If you don't have a place you regularly use when you are job hunting, skip the questions related to your job-hunting space.

Rate the following according to this scale:

1 = Usually neat, clean, and well-organized.
2 = A bit cluttered; I can usually find things pretty easily.
3 = Medium cluttered; I could definitely use some help.
4 = Pretty messy; finding things is pretty difficult.
5 = In danger of being declared a federal disaster area.
N/A = Not applicable

Job-Hunting Space	1	2	3	4	5	N/A
Overall appearance of office						
Desktop						
Other horizontal surfaces						
Desk drawers						
File drawers						
Bookcase						
Computer files						
Computer desktop						
Briefcase						
Other (specify)						

Personal Spaces	1	2	3	4	5	N/A
Bedroom closet, dresser, other bedroom storage						
Bedroom horizontal surfaces						
Car						
Kitchen counters						
Kitchen cupboards						
Garage						
Basement						
Attic						
Purse/wallet						
Other household storage						
Most horizontal surfaces (including the floor)						
Other (specify)						

How long would it take you to find:	Under 10 seconds	Less than 3 minutes	More than 3 minutes	N/A
A stapler				
A blue or black pen (that works!)				
A red pen				
A paper clip				
A flash (USB storage) drive				
A sharp pencil (or mechanical one that's not empty)				
An email, paper, or electronic memo you need to consult				
A pair of scissors				
Other (specify)				

When it comes to tidying up your job-hunting space:

____ Everything has a place.
____ Most things have a place.
____ There's a fair amount of stuff that sits out because it doesn't have a place.
____ There's a large amount of stuff that sits out because it doesn't have a place.
____ N/A, I don't have a specific space where I do most of my job hunting.

When it comes to putting away the stuff in the rest of my environment:

____ Everything has a place.
____ Most things have a place.
____ There's a fair amount that sits out because it doesn't have a place.
____ There's a large amount that sits out because it doesn't have a place.

The main reason things in my job-hunting space don't have a place is:

____ I don't have enough space.
____ I have enough space, but I just never got around to assigning them a place.
____ N/A, most things in my job-hunting space have a place.
____ N/A, I have no dedicated job-hunting space.

The main reason things in the rest of my environment don't have a place is:

___ I don't have enough space.

___ I have enough space, but I just never got around to assigning them a place.

___ N/A, most things in my house have a place.

Do you use the surface of your job-hunting space for long-term storage (other than a few frequently used items like a pen/pencil holder, paperclip holder, etc.)?

___ I haven't seen the top of that surface in years.

___ Yes, I store a fair amount of things there.

___ I store a few things there that should probably be somewhere else.

___ I don't store anything on the top of my desk.

___ N/A, I have no dedicated job-hunting space.

What percentage of the surface of your job-hunting space can you see when you walk into the office most mornings?

___ 75–100%

___ 50–75%

___ 25–50%

___ 0–25%

___ N/A, I have no dedicated job-hunting office.

How easy/difficult is it to tidy up your job-hunting space?

___ Pretty easy.

___ Not too difficult, maybe a little challenging.

___ Pretty difficult, usually stuff just gets tossed out of sight.

___ Impossible, too much stuff, not enough storage, no organization.

___ N/A, I have no dedicated job-hunting space.

When I go to a place that is giving away freebies, I usually:

___ Take everything; I can't resist anything that's free, whether I need it or not.

___ Take more than I think I'll use, but often don't use most of it.

___ Take only what I think I'll use, but often don't use most of it.

___ Take only what I think I'll use, and usually use what I take.

How often do you end up purchasing something new because you can't find the one that you already own?

___ Often

___ Occasionally

___ Rarely or never

When I replace a piece of electronic equipment (computer, MP3 player, camera, etc.), I:

___ Get rid of the old one.

___ Usually get rid of the old one but sometimes keep it "just in case."

___ Have an electronic graveyard in my basement.

When it comes to keeping stuff, on a scale of 1–10 where

1 = "I get rid of everything I don't use and keep nothing out of sentiment," and
10 = "I keep everything; I could probably be on that TV show about hoarders,"

I would give myself a rating of: _____.

Regarding acquiring stuff, on a scale of 1–10 where

1 = "I work very hard not to acquire any more stuff in my life," and
10 = "I just love to shop, receive gifts, get free stuff, and generally acquire anything and everything,"

I would give myself a rating of: _____.

Overall, on a scale of 1–10 where

1 = "My stuff and space are completely under control," and
10 = "My stuff and space are completely out of control,"

I would give myself a rating of: _____.

Your Information Management

Being able to put your fingers on important information is crucial to an effective job search. Without good information organization, you can waste a lot of time looking up things that you have already looked up before. Whether or not you have a specific job-searching space, the state of your information is going to impact the search.

My to-do list is:

___ Organized, all in one or two places.

___ On little notes all over the place.

___ Non-existent.

I have the following piles in my home awaiting my attention:

___ Personal magazines and other personal reading

___ Professional magazines and other professional reading

___ Non-junk mail that I'm going to get to eventually

___ Junk mail and catalogs I want to go through

____ Paper that needs to be filed, recycled, or otherwise dealt with

____ Items that have been sitting around on tables, countertops, etc. for ages

____ Some stuff that should be tossed, like old drink cups and other disposables

____ Items that I'm currently working on

____ Very few or no piles

____ Piles everywhere (verging on hoarding)

___ Other: _____

Regarding paper junk mail:

____ I get a lot.

____ I get a little.

____ Junk mail slows me down when I go through my mail each day.

____ Junk mail does not take up much of my time.

____ Junk mail is adding significantly to the clutter in my house.

____ Junk mail is not a clutter problem for me.

____ I have opted out of junk mail (e.g., at websites such as *www.catalogchoice.org* or *www.DMAchoice.org*).

____ When I get an unwanted catalog, I go to the company's website and unsubscribe myself from their mailing list.

What do you do with junk mail that comes to your home?

____ Save most of it to look at someday.

____ Recycle most of it immediately.

____ Read what is useful in a timely fashion and recycle the rest.

___ Other: _____

Which most closely describes your paper magazine, newspaper, and other personal and professional subscriptions?

____ I'm generally caught up on my reading.

____ I usually read all of the periodicals I subscribe to before the next one arrives.

____ I have subscriptions I plan to eventually read.

____ I'm a bit behind on my reading.

____ I'm hopelessly behind on my reading.

____ I have subscriptions I know I'll never get to.

____ N/A, I don't have any paper subscriptions. Skip the next question.

When I'm finished with a paper magazine or other periodical, I:

____ Put it in a pile with other old periodicals.

____ Recycle the whole thing.

___ Cut out and file—or scan—anything I'll want to refer to later, then recycle the rest.

___ Cut out anything I want to refer to later, stick it on a pile somewhere, then recycle the rest.

___ Rarely get around to finishing magazines, so they stack up.

___ Other: _____.

My file drawers are:

___ Mostly organized.

___ Not full and have space for additional filing.

___ Jammed full.

___ Mostly disorganized.

___ Full of stuff that I'll probably never need again.

___ Filled with files I might need but rarely use that are taking up prime filing space instead of being archived elsewhere.

___ A total disaster.

When a brilliant idea strikes me, I:

___ Write it down so I don't forget it, but I usually can't find it later.

___ Write it down so I don't forget it; I know exactly where it is.

___ Usually successfully remember it without writing it down.

___ Usually try to remember it, but usually forget it.

When I go to a job fair, meeting, or conference, I usually:

___ Take a bunch of handouts but never look at them.

___ Take a bunch of handouts, look over them, and discard the ones I don't want.

___ Take a bunch of handouts and read them all.

___ Take a few handouts and read most of the ones that I take.

___ Take a few handouts but usually don't get to most of them.

The information I have on my personal computer is mostly:

___ Extremely important.

___ Pretty important.

___ Somewhat important.

___ Not at all important.

I back up my computer files:

____ Daily or more often.

____ At least once a week.

____ At least once a month.

____ Never.

____ I use an automated backup system, so I don't have to worry about this.

My passwords for my online accounts are:

____ The same for each account.

____ Something simple to guess, like my first name or birthday.

____ Trickier to guess, but not as secure as they could be.

____ Different for each account.

____ The same for some accounts, but different for other accounts.

____ A combination of upper and lower case letters, numbers, and symbols.

____ I keep a master copy of my passwords in a safe place, for disaster recovery purposes.

Regarding email:

____ I check out every email that comes into my email box, including junk mail, jokes, etc.

____ I usually quickly delete spam, jokes, etc. without reading.

____ I have a good spam filter.

____ I spend about the right amount of time on my email.

____ I spend too much time on my email.

____ My email time is way out of control.

Regarding paper:

____ My paper is under control.

____ My paper is somewhat out of control.

____ Help! I'm buried in paper!

The business cards that people give me are:

____ All over the place.

____ In one specific place but not sorted.

____ Sorted and filed, or scanned/entered into the computer.

____ Other: _____.

Overall, on a scale of 1–10 where

1 = "My information is completely under control," and
10 = "My information is completely out of control,"

I would give myself a rating of: _____ .

Your Personal Wellness

Sleep

How much sleep do you generally get on weeknights?

___ Less than 4 hours
___ 4–5 hours
___ 6–7 hours
___ More than 7 hours

How much sleep do you generally get on weekend nights?

___ Less than 4 hours
___ 4–5 hours
___ 6–7 hours
___ More than 7 hours

How much sleep do you feel you actually need?

___ 5–6 hours
___ 7–8 hours
___ More than 8 hours
___ I have no idea.

Do you usually go to bed at the same time each night?

___ No, it often varies.
___ Yes, on weekdays, but I stay up later on weekends and sleep in.
___ Yes, but I wake up at a different time on weekends vs. weekdays.
___ Yes, I go to bed close to the same time every night, and get up close to the same time every morning (give or take an hour).

How long does it usually take you to fall asleep after you turn off the lights?

___ Less than 15 minutes
___ 15–30 minutes
___ More than 30 minutes

How often do you usually wake up in the middle of the night?

____ Never

____ 1–2 times

____ 3 or more times

When I wake up in the middle of the night, I:

____ Generally get back to sleep quickly.

____ Lie awake for 20 minutes or more.

____ Get out of bed if I can't get back to sleep.

I watch television, or use the computer, within 2 hours of bedtime:

____ Often.

____ Occasionally.

____ Rarely or never.

I have an alcoholic drink within 3 hours of bedtime:

____ Often.

____ Occasionally.

____ Rarely or never.

I intentionally nap (as opposed to unintentionally nodding off):

____ Often.

____ Occasionally.

____ Rarely or never.

I nod off during the day:

____ Often.

____ Occasionally.

____ Rarely or never.

Regarding my tiredness level during the day:

____ I'm really tired; I often have a hard time making it through the day.

____ I'm generally tired but functioning.

____ I'm sometimes tired; it's not a problem overall.

____ I'm rarely tired; I feel rested in general.

Physical Fitness

I usually do cardiovascular exercise:

___ Regularly, ___ times per week.
___ Occasionally.
___ Rarely or never.

I usually do strength training:

___ Regularly, ___ times per week.
___ Occasionally.
___ Rarely or never.

I usually do stretching exercises:

___ Regularly, ___ times per week.
___ Occasionally.
___ Rarely or never.

Eating Habits

Which of these unhealthy eating habits apply to you?

I eat processed and prepared foods:

___ Often.
___ Occasionally.
___ Rarely or never.

I eat out or order take-out:

___ Often.
___ Occasionally.
___ Rarely or never.

I drink soda (either diet or regular):

___ Often.
___ Occasionally.
___ Rarely or never.

I drink more than 2 cups/day of coffee:

___ Often.
___ Occasionally.
___ Rarely or never.

I eat high-fat foods:

___ Often.
___ Occasionally.
___ Rarely or never.

I eat sugary foods:

___ Often.
___ Occasionally.
___ Rarely or never.

I sit in front of the TV or computer and unconsciously snack:

___ Often.
___ Occasionally.
___ Rarely or never.

I tend to grab whatever is handy to eat:

___ Often.
___ Occasionally.
___ Rarely or never.

I skip breakfast, or just have a cup of coffee:

___ Often.
___ Occasionally.
___ Rarely or never.

I eat something sweet and/or highly processed for breakfast:

___ Often.
___ Occasionally.
___ Rarely or never.

Which of these **healthy** eating habits apply to you?

I eat fresh vegetables and fruits:

___ Often.
___ Occasionally.
___ Rarely or never.

I tend to eat whole grains instead of refined grains:

___ Often.
___ Occasionally.
___ Rarely or never.

Most of what I eat is prepared from scratch:

___ Often.
___ Occasionally.
___ Rarely or never.

I try to drink water to stay hydrated throughout the day:

___ Often.
___ Occasionally.
___ Rarely or never.

I take vitamins, minerals, and other supplements:

___ Often.
___ Occasionally.
___ Rarely or never.

I eat a good breakfast:

___ Often.
___ Occasionally.
___ Rarely or never.

Overall, I'd say my diet and eating habits are:

___ Very healthy.
___ Pretty healthy.
___ Fair.
___ Pretty unhealthy.
___ Terrible.

Other

The last time I had a checkup, my doctor told me to:

____ Lose weight.
____ Stop smoking.
____ Lower my alcohol intake.
____ Lower my caffeine intake.
____ Lower my sodium intake.
____ Exercise more.
____ Lower my stress level.
____ Change my diet in some way (specify): _____.
____ Other: _____.
____ I haven't had a checkup in years.

I take time for activities that nurture me (hobbies, meditation, hot bath, etc.):

____ At least once per week.
____ At least once per month.
____ Rarely.
____ Never.

Have you been experiencing any of the following symptoms for most of the day, and nearly every day, for at least two weeks?

____ Persistent sad, anxious, or "empty" mood
____ Feelings of hopelessness, or pessimism
____ Irritability
____ Feelings of guilt, worthlessness, or helplessness
____ Loss of interest or pleasure in hobbies and activities
____ Decreased energy or fatigue
____ Moving or talking more slowly
____ Feeling restless or having trouble sitting still
____ Difficulty concentrating, remembering, or making decisions
____ Difficulty sleeping, early-morning awakening, or oversleeping
____ Appetite and/or weight changes
____ Thoughts of death or suicide, or suicide plans/attempts
____ Aches or pains, headaches, cramps, or digestive problems without a clear physical cause and/or that do not ease even with treatment

If you have checked one or more of the above, you may be suffering from depression.[?] This is not uncommon for people who are unemployed, or in the wrong job, or experiencing other life stressors. Please talk to your doctor.

Overall, on a scale of 1–10 where

1 = "I live a very healthy lifestyle," and
10 = "I live a very unhealthy lifestyle,"

I would give myself a rating of: _____.

Overall, on a scale of 1–10 where

1 = "I feel great most of the time," and
10 = "I feel terrible most of the time,"

I would give myself a rating of: _____.

Appendix B:
Getting Control of Your Environment

If your working space is such a disaster that it's holding up your job search, you need to get it under control. Fast. But most people don't have a clue how to organize without getting bogged down in the project.

The Typical Approach

This is the way most people approach cleaning up a messy desk: select an item, and decide whether to keep it or get rid of it. If they are going to keep it, they have to decide where it's going to go, or else put it in a "keep" pile to decide later. Often they'll find a paper or a book that interests them and get lost in reading it.

After a while, it seems that the desk isn't getting any emptier, but time is passing. Finally, they give up, throw everything back on the desk, and walk away in disgust, thinking maybe they'll come back to it another day when they have more time or energy. Does that sound familiar?

Divide and Conquer

I advocate a different approach to organizing any disorganized area. First, get some (8–10, perhaps) of these nice Sterilite® 66-Quart Latch™ Boxes. I particularly like these boxes because they're sturdy, stack-able, and transparent. Heavy cardboard boxes with lids are not quite as good, but they work okay and are usually free. For a task like this, I like the ones you can pick up at a liquor store, because they are made to hold a lot of weight and they usually come with lids. You can, of course, get them from the store either empty or full!

Next, choose a manageable space (say, a desk, or a cabinet), and quickly empty everything from your space into the boxes. Make no decisions yet about what to do with each item—just throw it in. The only exception is to keep aside anything you're going to need in the next couple of weeks. When a box fills up, stack it on the previous one and then start filling up the next box. Continue doing this until the entire space is clear.

At this point, you've already accomplished three things:

- You've broken the problem down into discrete units (the boxes), and can go through the items one box at a time. Although the space was overwhelming as a whole, each box is pretty manageable.
- You've reduced the footprint of the mess by stacking the boxes to give yourself breathing room.
- The space is now a clean slate. Instead of trying to organize a messy area, you are working with a clean space.

But here's a warning if you use this method: do NOT empty that space into those boxes unless you have a plan for actually emptying the boxes. Otherwise, I guarantee you you'll be dead and gone, and those boxes will still be full of that stuff! So, plan to set aside some time—maybe just 10 minutes each day or an hour each Saturday—to work your way through the boxes.

Now you can start organizing the space from scratch. Maybe buy some stacking trays or containers to hold things. Then, start going through the storage boxes, getting rid of stuff you no longer need or want, and methodically putting things you want to keep into their new homes.

And, by the way, it's essential to have empty file drawer space for papers you decide to keep. You won't get very far without file drawer space. Too often, papers are stacked in piles on top of desks because drawers are full to bursting. If that's your problem, either get some new file cabinets, or buy some long-term storage cardboard "bankers boxes," at your local office supply store. Archive files in them that you haven't looked at for years. Mark the date you put them in storage, and place them in the basement, attic, garage, or somewhere else—other than in your active work space. You can go through them more closely at a later date.

Appendix C:
What Are American Job Centers?

American Job Centers (also known as One-Stop Career Centers, or "One-Stops") are funded through the U.S. Department of Labor and "are designed to provide a full range of assistance to job seekers under one roof…[T]he centers offer training referrals, career counseling, job listings, and similar employment-related services. Customers can visit a center in person or connect to the center's information online or through kiosk remote access."[10]

Who Do They Help?

One-Stops provide services for nearly everyone:
- Career changers
- Veterans
- Laid-off workers
- Entry-level workers
- Young adults
- Older workers
- Workers with disabilities
- Workers with a criminal record
- Credential seekers

What Do They Do?

The staff at the One-Stops can provide assistance to get you through the entire job-search process. In addition, their website, *www.careeronestop.org*, provides plenty of online resources. But don't limit yourself to only what you can find on the Internet. Find a local office under the "Find Local Help" tab on the One-Stop homepage and give them a call. After you fill out an application and attend an introductory meeting, you will speak with an experienced job counselor who will address your individual needs and guide you through the job-search process. In addition, you can take workshops on everything from résumé writing, to interviewing skills, to salary negotiation, and lots of things in between. The following are some of the ways your One-Stop will help you.

Find the Right Job

It's important to look for a job that fits you well. If needed, the counselors at your One-Stop can administer assessments that can help you learn more about your interests and aptitudes. They can help you figure out what skills you bring to a job, and also if you need more training or experience. You can find out about careers you would like and are a good match for your personality, but which you might not have considered before.

Explore Careers

Once you know what are the best careers for you, your job specialist can help you learn more about those careers. In addition, they can point you toward appropriate job openings. They can point you toward more training or education, if needed, and even help you find scholarships and grants to pay for it. If you have lost a job because it's become obsolete (think: telephone operator, etc), your job specialist will help you to identify skills that you have from your former job that will transfer to a new career. In addition, you can find out about whether the long-term prospects in a particular occupation are growing or shrinking.

What Else?

Your One-Stop can let you know about upcoming job fairs. Résumé writers will help you put together your résumé and cover letters so that you stand above the crowd of applicants. You'll learn how to maximize the effectiveness of your LinkedIn profile, and also how to use LinkedIn to your greatest advantage. By taking workshops on job interviewing, you will learn how you come across in an interview and how to put your best foot forward—and how to field the most difficult questions. Once you have a job offer, they can help you negotiate compensation.

What Does It Cost?

In many One-Stops, services are free to all job seekers. However, this can vary from state to state and even office to office. There may also be some income requirements to be eligible for certain programs, especially those provided in partnership with third parties. You may have to pay for training or education, but your One-Stop can help you find scholarships and financial aid. Check with your local One-Stop to verify free and low-cost services.

Don't Judge a Book...

Job seekers with advanced degrees on professional career tracks often think that the One-Stops are only for people looking for service and trade jobs. However nothing could be further from the truth. They work with people from all walks of life. There are many clients seeking high-level positions, along with those looking for blue-collar and labor jobs. The people at the centers are highly trained and experienced in dealing with all levels of employment. Their main priority is helping people find the appropriate match for their skills, aptitudes, and interests.

Appendix D:
What Are Vocational
Rehabilitation Centers?

State Vocational Rehabilitation Centers (VRCs) provide employment assistance to individuals with physical, intellectual, or emotional disabilities. According to one website, "The Vocational Rehabilitation Program helps individuals with physical, psychiatric and/or learning disabilities face the challenges of the modern workplace. This may include identifying job goals based on individual interests and aptitudes, providing funds for college and vocational training, assessing worksite accommodations, educating an employer about the Americans with Disabilities Act, or assisting an individual returning to work after adjusting to a new disabling condition." [11]

In short, VRCs can help you navigate barriers to employment. Their goal is to help clients get on the road to economic self-sufficiency. Most clients will enter the workplace in entry-level jobs with potential for growth and advancement.

The most valuable service that VRCs provide is counseling and guidance—which is offered at no charge to anyone with a disability. VRC staff can also connect job seekers with other appropriate agencies, such as organizations offering assistance to people with physical, mental, or emotional impairments.[11]

VRCs help people find jobs in all sectors, from labor and service to professional and white-collar jobs. The services provided are free to all job seekers with an ADA-recognized disability—although certain services, such as training, education, and third-party services (such as evaluations) may require payment. If additional supports are needed, job counselors can help determine eligibility for financial assistance. In many states, VRCs provide some tuition funding for eligible clients.

Who Is Eligible?

Anyone with a physical, psychiatric, or learning disability that significantly affects their ability to get and keep a job is eligible for services at a VRC. The disability must be documented by a licensed professional. A disability, no matter how severe, that does not interfere with a person's ability to work in a chosen profession would not count. For example, a computer programmer with a prosthetic leg would not be eligible for VRC services since most commercial buildings are ADA accessible. However, if that programmer only had one hand, he or she might need accommodations (specialized work equipment) in order to perform the job—and would then be eligible for VRC services.

How Does It Work?

Getting Started

In my state of Massachusetts, for example, you (or a support person of your choosing) contact your local Rehabilitation Commission office. After a brief interview by phone, TTY, or computer to determine eligibility for vocational services, you sign up for a group orientation session where they explain the services offered, what they can do to help you, and what your responsibilities are in the process. When the session is over, if you feel the VRC may be helpful in your job search, you complete a short application. In a few weeks, they'll contact you by mail with the name of your counselor, who you (or your support person) will contact to set up an initial appointment.

You will meet with your job counselor for an hour and are expected to bring supporting documentation about your disability, along with a completed informational sheet. Support people, such as family members, friends, or professionals such as a coaches, are welcome to participate.

After meeting with your job counselor, you may apply for services if you feel that they will be helpful to you. You will be formally notified as to whether you are eligible for services within several weeks of submitting your application and documentation.

Assessment

Your counselor will conduct vocational assessments to help determine what services will need to be provided for the jobs you seek. He or she will consider your interests, abilities, education, aptitudes, work history, disabilities, and other pertinent information. You may also participate in vocational testing to help determine what careers are appropriate for you. In all cases, only jobs with a realistic probability of success will be considered. Job categories with few openings, or those that are highly competitive (such as video game designer) are not usually considered appropriate career goals. The aim is to find a sustainable path to economic independence, not a "dream job"—although the two are not necessarily mutually exclusive.

Creating the Plan

Once all the data has been collected and analyzed, you and your counselor will create an Individual Plan for Employment (IPE). This will specify your career goal, list your responsibilities for the career search (clients are expected to be active participants in the search process), and outline services the VRC will provide to help you become employed.

You will meet with your counselor regularly to review the process and consider any modifications or additions to the IPE. If you run into any snags along the way, your counselor is available and can help you figure out a solution to keep you on the path towards employment. He or she will also help you find—and sign up for—any additional training or education you may need.

What Else?

Once your plan is completed, you will also work with a job placement specialist to find open positions in your chosen field. The job placement specialist will help you decide if a particular opening is appropriate for you. He or she will also help with the application process, if needed.

The counselors at your local Vocational Rehabilitation Center can help you with résumé preparation and interview training. There are specialists who can help you determine if earning income will affect benefits—such as Supplemental Social Security Income and Social Security Disability Insurance. Your counselor can help you figure out what reasonable accommodations may be needed to help you perform the essential functions of your job. Your VRC may also encourage an evaluation to see if job-related assistive technology would be appropriate for you. If so, they can assist you in obtaining that additional support. Once you are employed, the VRC staff is still available to help you navigate any difficulties with the new job.

What Are the Results?

Here is some feedback from clients, as listed in The Massachusetts Rehabilitation Commission's *Consumer Handbook:*[12]

> "With assistance from MRC I was able to get the services I needed and receive the education and training that I wanted. I now have a job that I love and am in the process of applying for grad school. Thank you MRC."

> "The help I received was very significant and targeted to improving my employability. It helped and made a difference positively—much more so than I expected."

> "MRC is very helpful for people who have a disability—are understanding, kind, have a lot of patience. They find the right job for you according to your disability and if you have a hard time at your job they will help you."

The information provided in this chapter came from the Massachusetts Rehabilitation Commission. Although there will be some variations from state to state, you will find this information will be pretty similar at all of the vocational rehabilitation offices throughout the country. To find your local vocational rehabilitation office, search the Internet using the terms "Vocational Rehabilitation [Your_State_Name]."

Appendix E:
Résumé Worksheet†

B efore sitting in front of a computer to compose your résumé, it may be very beneficial to capture all your thoughts down on paper first. Starting this document from scratch can be a very overwhelming experience so we recommend creating a first draft by hand. This worksheet will help you capture all your needed information. Once complete, you can deal with formatting your résumé on a computer using a word processing software package, such as Microsoft Word.

Contact information *(this will become your header)*

Name: _____

Current Address: _____

City/State/Zip: _____

Telephone #: _____

E-mail address: _____

LinkedIn Address: _____
(If Applicable)

Professional Summary

In a few sentences (or bullet points) summarize your professional qualifications. This may include years of experience, key transferable skills, and/or major accomplishments.

_____

_____

_____

† Used by permission of the North Shore Career Center, Salem, MA.

Work Experience

List your jobs, beginning with your most recent one. We recommend listing only the last 10–15 years of work experience. Every listed job and accompanying responsibilities should be applicable toward the job your are applying for. Use job descriptions to find industry words and key phrases.

Company: _____   Dates Employed: _____

City/State: _____   Job Title: _____

Key accomplishments and responsibilities:

_____

_____

_____

_____

_____

Company: _____   Dates Employed: _____

City/State: _____   Job Title: _____

Key accomplishments and responsibilities:

_____

_____

_____

_____

_____

Appendix E: Résumé Worksheet

Company: _____   Dates Employed: _____

City/State: _____   Job Title: _____

Key accomplishments and responsibilities:

_____

_____

_____

_____

_____

_____

Company: _____   Dates Employed: _____

City/State: _____   Job Title: _____

Key accomplishments and responsibilities:

_____

_____

_____

_____

_____

_____

Education

Beginning with your highest level of education, list colleges/universities, vocational schools, and/or high schools you attended.

Name of School: _____

City/State: _____

Degree/Diploma: _____

Major/Coursework: _____

Name of School: _____

City/State: _____

Degree/Diploma: _____

Major/Coursework: _____

Name of School: _____

City/State: _____

Degree/Diploma: _____

Major/Coursework: _____

Volunteer Experience

Your gainful work may not be the only source of experience to show you are qualified for the job you are applying for. If you have volunteered, or are currently volunteering, it can work in your favor to show on your résumé how you have been giving back, if it shows job-related interests and skills. Many companies make it a point to demonstrate their community involvement. Therefore, they like to see any job-relevant community involvement on a job seeker's résumé as well.

Organization: _____   Dates Volunteered: _____

City/State: _____

Job Title: _____

Key accomplishments and responsibilities:

_____

_____

_____

_____

_____

Professional Credentials

Include information about foreign language skills, computer/technical certifications, professional memberships/organizations you belong to, and other relevant certifications and/or licenses. Ensure that anything you list is applicable to the job you are applying for.

_____

_____

_____

_____

_____

_____

Appendix F:
Online Job Boards

Use this list of websites to find openings in your area, or get an idea of the kind of jobs that might be of interest to you. I have included a description of websites, mostly from the websites themselves. There are many other online job boards out there as well, especially in specialized job sectors; just do a little research to ensure they are legitimate. If they require a fee to search the site, move on. There are plenty of good job boards that you can use for free. These are just a few of them.

Please note, however, that very few people find work by submitting applications through online job boards. The statistics are not in your favor. Very few applications survive the filtering process, and most people never hear anything after hitting "submit." That said, job boards can be helpful for researching companies and comparing positions, and you might get lucky when submitting an application. It never hurts to apply but just keep expectations realistic. An in-depth discussion of job board best practices is beyond the scope of this book, but it may be worth doing some online research to maximize your chances of success.

General Websites

The following websites contain jobs of all levels and from all hiring sectors of the country, and many have international postings as well. If you are not sure about what's out there and what kind of jobs might appeal to you, these can be a great place to do research. In addition, you can learn about what kinds of training and experience you need for specific jobs.

Career Builder *www.careerbuilder.org* "CareerBuilder is a global, end-to-end human capital solutions company focused on helping employers find, hire and manage great talent. Optimized for any device, we make it easy for people to find and apply to your jobs, while providing powerful insights to keep applicants engaged."[13]

Glassdoor *www.glassdoor.com* "Glassdoor holds a growing database of millions of company reviews, CEO approval ratings, salary reports, interview reviews and questions, benefits reviews, office photos and more. Unlike other jobs sites, all of this information is entirely shared by those who know a company best—the employees. Add to that millions of the latest jobs—no other site allows you to see which employers are hiring, what it's really like to work or interview there according to employees, and how much you could earn."[14]

Indeed *www.indeed.com* "As the world's #1 job site, with over 200 million unique visitors every month from over 60 different countries, Indeed has become the catalyst for putting the world to work. Indeed is intensely passionate about delivering the right fit for every hire. Indeed helps companies of all sizes hire the best talent and offers the best opportunity for job seekers to get hired."[15]

LinkUp *www.linkup.com* "Completely unique in the industry, LinkUp is the only job search engine that indexes jobs exclusively from company websites. Updated daily, the 3+ million jobs in our search engine are always current with no duplicates or job pollution… As a result, we deliver a phenomenal user experience for job seekers and a terrific value proposition for our employer advertisers and data clients."[16]

Monster *www.monster.com* "Monster is a global online employment solution for people seeking jobs and the employers who need great people. We've been doing this for more than 20 years, and have expanded from our roots as a 'job board' to a global provider of a full array of job seeking, career management, recruitment and talent management products and services."[17]

Simply Hired *www.simplyhired.com* "Learn about and find jobs in each city's most popular industries, top companies, and job types. View detailed salary information for thousands of different careers. Search by job title or location, compare job offers, or plot your current salary against local and national averages."[18]

Snagajob *www.snagajob.com* "With more than 75 million registered hourly workers and 300,000 employer locations, Snagajob is America's #1 hourly marketplace. We focus on creating instant and quality connections so workers can get jobs and employers can hire workers—in minutes. Since 2000, our mission has been to put people in right fit-positions so they can maximize their potential and live more fulfilling lives. We do this through the Snagajob marketplace and PeopleMatter, our end-to-end platform of talent and workforce management solutions."[19]

Targeted Websites

The following websites are for people who already have specific job or career objectives.

Advertising

Talent Zoo *www.talentzoo.com* "Welcome to the best site in the galaxy for advertising jobs. Whether you're seeking a creative, media planning/buying, production, design, account management or interactive job opportunity, you're in the right place. Upload your resume or portfolio and apply to great advertising jobs today."[20]

Current college students and recent college graduates

College Recruiter *CollegeRecruiter.com* "At College Recruiter, we believe that every student and recent grad deserves a great career. We believe in creating a great candidate and recruiter experience. Our interactive media solutions connect students and grads to great careers."[21]

Design

Talent Zoo *www.talentzoo.com* "Welcome to your one-stop shop on the web for creative jobs, design jobs, web jobs, career advice and much more. Get started now and find creative jobs in design, tech, new media and traditional media posted by agencies, recruiters, corporate and start-ups."[22]

Education, elementary and secondary

SchoolSpring *www.schoolspring.com* "Whether you're just starting out or you're experienced, SchoolSpring is the best place to manage your education career. Access thousands of job openings nationwide from all over the Web in a single, easy-to-search engine."[23]

Education, post-secondary

HigherEdJobs *www.higheredjobs.com* "HigherEdJobs is the leading source for jobs and career information in academia. More colleges and universities trust HigherEdJobs to recruit faculty and administrators than any other source. Each month our site is visited by more than one million higher education professionals who rely not only on our comprehensive list of jobs, but also on our news and career advice."[24]

Entry level

Job-Applications.com *www.entryleveljobs.net* "Looking for entry-level jobs has never been easier than it is when you use Local.Job-Applications.com. We show applicants jobs in every major industry and with the most sought-after employers, searchable by city or state. With available postings all in one place, job seekers can avoid endless searching trying to find their next place of employment. Instead, see who's hiring locally all from the convenience of your laptop or smart phone. With Local.Job-Applications.com, finding your next job is only a click away."[25]

Federal government

USAJOBS *www.usajobs.gov* "USAJOBS connects job seekers with federal employment opportunities across the United States and around the world. As the Federal Government's official employment site, USAJOBS provides resources to help the right people find the right jobs."[26]

Finance

eFinancialCareers *www.efinancialcareers.com* "If you're a financial professional, we'll give you the vital edge you need to maximize your career. Invaluable industry insights, for example. Access to career-changing roles from across the industry from leading brands to niche boutiques. Not to mention news and analysis, career-shaping advice and professional opinion. In short, we focus on helping you be first in line, and best prepared. We make sure you know about the latest opportunities and have the best market intelligence—wherever and whenever you need it."[27]

OneWire *www.onewire.com* "At OneWire, we are dedicated to creating a platform where finance professionals can confidentially connect with top industry employers. In 2008, we founded OneWire with the goal to introduce the power and ease of technology into the finance recruitment space. Candidates on OneWire can actively apply to jobs, follow companies and advance their career with exclusive career-specific content."[28]

Flexible

FlexJobs *www.FlexJobs.com* "FlexJobs knows that there's a ton of junk out there for job seekers. Whether it's the too-good-to-be-true business opportunities, endless ads, broken links, repetitive postings, or just straight-out scams... well, yes, there's a lot of junk out there. And it's often burying the actual good job opportunities. FlexJobs can change that. We can make your job search experience better, easier, faster, and safer."[29]

Food industry

Good Food Jobs *www.goodfoodjobs.com* "Good Food Jobs is a gastro-job search tool, designed to link people looking for meaningful food work with the businesses that need their energy, enthusiasm, and intellect. We post opportunities with farmers and food artisans, policy makers and purveyors, retailers and restaurateurs, economists, ecologists, and more. On our blog, the gastrognomes, we profile the most interesting and unlikely food professionals that we find, and publish their stories to inspire you."[30]

Health care

HealthcareJobsite *www.HealthcareJobsite.com* "HealthcareJobsite contains over 500,000 opportunities in a broad range of support, technician, nursing and physician roles within the healthcare sector. Registrants can incorporate work samples into their profile to provide employers with tangible evidence of past accomplishments."[31]

Marketing

Talent Zoo *www.talentzoo.com* "Begin your search now for not only great marketing jobs and PR jobs from across the nation but also valuable career advice to help you become more successful and fulfilled in your field. Companies of all shapes and sizes post marketing jobs on Talent Zoo in varied sectors including brand management, direct response marketing, digital marketing, tech, research, and management."[32]

Media

Mediabistro *www.mediabistro.com* "Find your next career opportunity. Browse all the media job openings below. Apply to the best jobs in marketing, advertising, publishing, sales, PR, digital media, television, design, and more."[33]

Outdoor

CoolWorks *www.coolworks.com* "Since 1995, CoolWorks has been a leader in connecting people seeking meaningful and exciting work with the employers who are looking for their enthusiasm, energy, and knowledge. We believe that you can and should love your job, and we want to help make that happen! We feature job opportunities in great places—from national parks to ski resorts, dude ranches to retreat centers, and everything in between."[34]

Sales

SalesJobs.com *www.SalesJobs.com* "Launched in June of 1997 during the nascent years of the Internet, SalesJobs.com has taken its place in history as the very first niche sales employment site and today SalesJobs.com dominates the sales employment industry commanding over 90% of the online sales employment market. SalesJobs.com is the worlds' oldest and largest sales employment site, with more sales jobs than all of our niche competitors combined worldwide."[35]

State, local government

Search for "[your state] government jobs" to find sites that show local, state and federal job openings in your area.

Student internships

Internships.com *www.internships.com* "Internships.com, a Chegg service, is the world's largest student-focused internship marketplace, bringing students, employers and higher education institutions together in one centralized location. Internships.com provides a wide variety of interactive tools and services to enable every student, employer and educator to better understand and optimize internship opportunities, enabling businesses to identify the best job candidates and for students to develop the real-world skills they will need upon graduation."[36]

Technical

Dice *www.dice.com* "We are organizing the world's talent by providing specialized insights and relevant connections tailored to specific professions and industries. Today, we serve: Technology, Security-Clearance, Financial Services, Energy, Healthcare, Hospitality."[37]

Talent Zoo *www.talentzoo.com* "Welcome to TalentZoo.com, your online resource for the best tech, digital, and web jobs around. From Design to Development to Social Media, we're your one stop shop."[38]

Volunteer positions and internships with nonprofits

Idealist *www.idealist.com* "Idealist is all about connecting idealists—people who want to do good—with opportunities for action and collaboration. With more than 120,000 organizations and 1.4 million monthly visitors to our English, and Spanish *(idealistas.org)* sites, Idealist helps people move from intention to action all over the world."[39]

Appendix G:
Labor Market Information (LMI):
Research Worksheet†

Goal: Labor market information (LMI) are tools to help you make decisions about your job search. While conducting a job search, this research is critical to understanding if there are employers seeking your skills, where the jobs are located, and what are the comparable wages in your desired industry. Completing this worksheet will help you make employment decisions about your current skills and industry.

Sources/Websites: There are various sources of labor market information that can be utilized and are found below.

- O*Net   www.onetonline.org
- America's Career Information Network   www.careerinfonet.org/occ_intro.asp
- US Bureau of Labor & Statistics   www.bls.gov
- My Skills My Future   www.myskillsmyfuture.org
- My Next Move   www.mynextmove.org

Please fill out the information below based on your research:

1) Desired job title: _____

2) What is the salary range? $_____ to $_____

3) Are opportunities in this occupation for the state and/or local market

       a. Increasing by _____ % **or**

       b. Decreasing by _____ %

4) How many jobs are available annually in this occupation? _____

---

† Used by permission of the North Shore Career Center, Salem, MA.

5) Based on your research do you possess the appropriate certifications, licenses, or credentials for this occupation? If your answer is **NO**, please identify which you lack to gain employment in this desired field.

6) Up to this point, why do you think you have been unable to become employed in this desired field?

Appendix H:
Time Wall Actions

One-Time Tasks

Career Path	Career Path	Career Path	Career Path
Complete the *Labor Market Information Research Worksheet* (Appendix G) to confirm that there are realistic hiring prospects for my desired position.	Confirm whether or not I currently have the background for my desired position.	If I don't have the needed background, determine what I need to do to get it.	Find out what other positions I might be qualified for.
Career Path	**Career Path**	**Career Path**	**Support**
Decide on the job sector(s) I want to work for.	Assess my skills that might transfer to other types of jobs.	Consider my personal branding. ("What do I bring to the party that is unique?")	Find career centers in my area.
Support	**Support**	**Support**	**Support**
Explore services offered by my local career center.	Register for relevant workshops and services offered by my local career center.	Sign up for assessments as needed: __ Skill levels __ Aptitudes __ Interests __ Abilities __ Myers-Briggs __ Other: _____	Look for counseling, articles, and workshops that address my concerns about age, having a criminal record, long gap in employment history, disability, or other perceived barriers to employment.
Support	**Support**	**Support**	**Unemployment Insurance**
Look for professional recruiters ("headhunters") who place candidates in my field.	Join or create a support group of job seekers that meets regularly.	Explore the possibility of working with a private career coach, life coach, or ADHD coach.	Determine if I'm eligible for unemployment benefits.
Unemployment Insurance	**Unemployment Insurance**	**Unemployment Insurance**	**Résumé, Etc.**
Find out what it takes to meet my state's requirements.	Apply for unemployment insurance benefits.	Decide on a way to keep track of job actions that satisfy the weekly check-in requirement.	Create or update a customizable master résumé.
Résumé, Etc.	**Résumé, Etc.**	**Résumé, Etc.**	**Networking**
Sign up for a résumé workshop or make an appointment with a résumé consultant to go over my résumé.	Create a master cover letter that I can customize for each job I apply to.	Ask 2-3 people to be references for me before I apply to any jobs.	Create a list of all of the people that I can contact, including their names, contact information, and my connection to them.
Networking	**Networking**	**Networking**	**Networking**
Volunteer as a way to widen my network, learn new skills, and give back.	Join relevant industry groups and professional organizations.	Create a website about my professional self.	Print business cards with my name, contact information, and areas of expertise.

LinkedIn	LinkedIn	LinkedIn	LinkedIn
Sign up for a class on using LinkedIn at a local career center, One-Stop, or online.	Complete my profile. Make sure it is current and well-written.	Join groups that are relevant to my career goals.	Write *sincere* recommendations for former supervisors, co-workers, clients, and other professional contacts.
LinkedIn	**LinkedIn**	**LinkedIn**	**Online Research**
Request former supervisors, co-workers, clients, and other professional contacts give me recommendations and endorsements.	Check my skills list and make sure it aligns with the skills needed for my desired job.	Prune any skills from my list that aren't relevant to my search.	Create a list of job boards that I want to search regularly. (See Appendix F, *Online Job Boards*, for ideas.)
Online Research	**Online Research**	**Online Research**	**Interviewing**
Make a list of target companies that I would like to work for to keep track of their openings.	Create an O*NET OnLine account at *https://www.onetonline.org*.	Check out my state's online job resources.	Explore places where I can get training and feedback to polish my skills.
Interviewing	**Interviewing**	**Interviewing**	**Interviewing**
Sign up for an interviewing workshop or coaching.	Join Toastmasters to learn to think on my feet and present myself well.	If I was fired, have a good (and honest) response for the question, "Why did you leave your previous position?"	Be prepared to answer other hard questions about myself that may come up in an interview.
Interviewing	**Education/Training**	**Education/Training**	**Education/Training**
Prepare quantifiable results to discuss during an interview E.g. "I consistently exceeded my weekly sales goals by 10–20%. "	Research the kinds of training, classes, or education needed for my career goals.	Find institutions that offer the education/training I need for my career goals.	Apply for education/training classes.
Education/Training	**Education/Training**	**Dealing with a Disability**	**Dealing with a Disability**
Research financial aid.	Brush up or learn new computer skills with online or in-person classes.	Find vocational rehabilitation centers in my area. (See Appendix D, *What Are Vocational Rehabilitation Centers*, for more information.)	Explore services offered by my local vocational rehabilitation center (VRC).
Dealing with a Disability	**Dealing with a Disability**	**Dealing with a Disability**	**Dealing with a Disability**
Register for relevant workshops and services offered by my local VRC.	Sign up for assessments as needed.	Learn about adaptive technology that might be needed to do my job.	Know what accommodations might be needed for me to do my desired job.
Other	**Other**	**Other**	**Other**

Schedule Regularly

Unemployment Insurance	**Unemployment Insurance**	**Unemployment Insurance**	**Unemployment Insurance**
Do the weekly mandatory online or in-person check-in.	Do the weekly mandatory online or in-person check-in.	Do the weekly mandatory online or in-person check-in.	Do the weekly mandatory online or in-person check-in.
Unemployment Insurance	**Unemployment Insurance**	**Unemployment Insurance**	**Unemployment Insurance**
Do the weekly mandatory online or in-person check-in.	Do the weekly mandatory online or in-person check-in.	Do the weekly mandatory online or in-person check-in.	Do the weekly mandatory online or in-person check-in.
Unemployment Insurance	**Unemployment Insurance**	**Unemployment Insurance**	**Unemployment Insurance**
Do the weekly mandatory online or in-person check-in.	Do the weekly mandatory online or in-person check-in.	Do the weekly mandatory online or in-person check-in.	Do the weekly mandatory online or in-person check-in.
Networking: People	**Networking: People**	**Networking: People**	**Networking: People**
Contact at least ____ people on the list each week, make notes about each contact.	Contact at least ____ people on the list each week, make notes about each contact.	Contact at least ____ people on the list each week, make notes about each contact.	Contact at least ____ people on the list each week, make notes about each contact.
Networking: People	**Networking: People**	**Networking: People**	**Networking: People**
Contact at least ____ people on the list each week, make notes about each contact.	Contact at least ____ people on the list each week, make notes about each contact.	Contact at least ____ people on the list each week, make notes about each contact.	Contact at least ____ people on the list each week, make notes about each contact.
Networking: People	**Networking: People**	**Networking: People**	**Networking: People**
Contact at least ____ people on the list each week, make notes about each contact.	Contact at least ____ people on the list each week, make notes about each contact.	Contact at least ____ people on the list each week, make notes about each contact.	Contact at least ____ people on the list each week, make notes about each contact.
Networking: Groups	**Networking: Groups**	**Networking: Groups**	**Networking: Groups**
Participate in relevant networking groups online, including LinkedIn, Facebook, and Twitter ____ times each week.	Participate in relevant networking groups online, including LinkedIn, Facebook, and Twitter ____ times each week.	Participate in relevant networking groups online, including LinkedIn, Facebook, and Twitter ____ times each week.	Participate in relevant networking groups online, including LinkedIn, Facebook, and Twitter ____ times each week.
Networking: Groups	**Networking: Groups**	**Networking: Groups**	**Networking: Groups**
Participate in relevant networking groups online, including LinkedIn, Facebook, and Twitter ____ times each week.	Participate in relevant networking groups online, including LinkedIn, Facebook, and Twitter ____ times each week.	Participate in relevant networking groups online, including LinkedIn, Facebook, and Twitter ____ times each week.	Participate in relevant networking groups online, including LinkedIn, Facebook, and Twitter ____ times each week.
Networking: Groups	**Networking: Groups**	**Networking: Groups**	**Networking: Groups**
Participate in relevant networking groups online, including LinkedIn, Facebook, and Twitter ____ times each week.	Participate in relevant networking groups online, including LinkedIn, Facebook, and Twitter ____ times each week.	Participate in relevant networking groups online, including LinkedIn, Facebook, and Twitter ____ times each week.	Participate in relevant networking groups online, including LinkedIn, Facebook, and Twitter ____ times each week

Networking: Email/BB	Networking: Email/BB	Networking: Email/BB	Networking: Email/BB
Participate in online discussion boards and email groups relevant to my professional interests ____ times each week.	Participate in online discussion boards and email groups relevant to my professional interests ____ times each week.	Participate in online discussion boards and email groups relevant to my professional interests ____ times each week.	Participate in online discussion boards and email groups relevant to my professional interests ____ times each week.
Networking: Email/BB	Networking: Email/BB	Networking: Email/BB	Networking: Email/BB
Participate in online discussion boards and email groups relevant to my professional interests ____ times each week.	Participate in online discussion boards and email groups relevant to my professional interests ____ times each week.	Participate in online discussion boards and email groups relevant to my professional interests ____ times each week.	Participate in online discussion boards and email groups relevant to my professional interests ____ times each week.
Networking: Email/BB	Networking: Email/BB	Networking: Email/BB	Networking: Email/BB
Participate in online discussion boards and email groups relevant to my professional interests ____ times each week.	Participate in online discussion boards and email groups relevant to my professional interests ____ times each week.	Participate in online discussion boards and email groups relevant to my professional interests ____ times each week.	Participate in online discussion boards and email groups relevant to my professional interests ____ times each week.
Networking: Interviews	Networking: Interviews	Networking: Interviews	Networking: Interviews
Set up informational interviews with people who have a position I aspire to.	Set up informational interviews with people who have a position I aspire to.	Set up informational interviews with people who have a position I aspire to.	Set up informational interviews with people who have a position I aspire to.
Networking: Interviews	Networking: Interviews	Networking: Interviews	Networking: Interviews
Set up informational interviews with people who have a position I aspire to.	Set up informational interviews with people who have a position I aspire to.	Set up informational interviews with people who have a position I aspire to.	Set up informational interviews with people who have a position I aspire to.
Networking: Interviews	Networking: Interviews	Networking: Interviews	Networking: Interviews
Set up informational interviews with people who have a position I aspire to.	Set up informational interviews with people who have a position I aspire to.	Set up informational interviews with people who have a position I aspire to.	Set up informational interviews with people who have a position I aspire to.
Networking: Functions	Networking: Functions	Networking: Functions	Networking: Functions
Attend industry group and professional organization functions to meet people face-to-face.	Attend industry group and professional organization functions to meet people face-to-face.	Attend industry group and professional organization functions to meet people face-to-face.	Attend industry group and professional organization functions to meet people face-to-face.
Networking: Functions	Networking: Functions	Networking: Functions	Networking: Functions
Attend industry group and professional organization functions to meet people face-to-face.	Attend industry group and professional organization functions to meet people face-to-face.	Attend industry group and professional organization functions to meet people face-to-face.	Attend industry group and professional organization functions to meet people face-to-face.

Networking: Functions	Networking: Functions	Networking: Functions	Networking: Functions
Attend industry group and professional organization functions to meet people face to face.	Attend industry group and professional organization functions to meet people face-to-face.	Attend industry group and professional organization functions to meet people face-to-face.	Attend industry group and professional organization functions to meet people face-to-face.
Networking: Meetings	Networking: Meetings	Networking: Meetings	Networking: Meetings
Attend networking meetings for fellow job seekers.	Attend networking meetings for fellow job seekers.	Attend networking meetings for fellow job seekers.	Attend networking meetings for fellow job seekers.
Networking: Meetings	Networking: Meetings	Networking: Meetings	Networking: Meetings
Attend networking meetings for fellow job seekers.	Attend networking meetings for fellow job seekers.	Attend networking meetings for fellow job seekers.	Attend networking meetings for fellow job seekers.
Networking: Meetings	Networking: Meetings	Networking: Meetings	Networking: Meetings
Attend networking meetings for fellow job seekers.	Attend networking meetings for fellow job seekers.	Attend networking meetings for fellow job seekers.	Attend networking meetings for fellow job seekers.
Networking: Events	Networking: Events	Networking: Events	Networking: Events
Attend social events that will expose me to new people to widen my network.	Attend social events that will expose me to new people to widen my network.	Attend social events that will expose me to new people to widen my network.	Attend social events that will expose me to new people to widen my network.
Networking: Events	Networking: Events	Networking: Events	Networking: Events
Attend social events that will expose me to new people to widen my network.	Attend social events that will expose me to new people to widen my network.	Attend social events that will expose me to new people to widen my network.	Attend social events that will expose me to new people to widen my network.
Networking: Events	Networking: Events	Networking: Events	Networking: Events
Attend social events that will expose me to new people to widen my network.	Attend social events that will expose me to new people to widen my network.	Attend social events that will expose me to new people to widen my network.	Attend social events that will expose me to new people to widen my network.
LinkedIn: Participate	LinkedIn: Participate	LinkedIn: Participate	LinkedIn: Participate
Comment on or initiate updates, shares, posts, and group conversations ___ times a week to keep my exposure high.	Comment on or initiate updates, shares, posts, and group conversations ___ times a week to keep my exposure high.	Comment on or initiate updates, shares, posts, and group conversations ___ times a week to keep my exposure high.	Comment on or initiate updates, shares, posts, and group conversations ___ times a week to keep my exposure high.
LinkedIn: Participate	LinkedIn: Participate	LinkedIn: Participate	LinkedIn: Participate
Comment on or initiate updates, shares, posts, and group conversations ___ times a week to keep my exposure high.	Comment on or initiate updates, shares, posts, and group conversations ___ times a week to keep my exposure high.	Comment on or initiate updates, shares, posts, and group conversations ___ times a week to keep my exposure high.	Comment on or initiate updates, shares, posts, and group conversations ___ times a week to keep my exposure high.

LinkedIn: Participate	LinkedIn: Participate	LinkedIn: Participate	LinkedIn: Participate
Comment on or initiate updates, shares, posts, and group conversations ___ times a week to keep my exposure high.	Comment on or initiate updates, shares, posts, and group conversations ___ times a week to keep my exposure high.	Comment on or initiate updates, shares, posts, and group conversations ___ times a week to keep my exposure high.	Comment on or initiate updates, shares, posts, and group conversations ___ times a week to keep my exposure high.
LinkedIn: Connect	LinkedIn: Connect	LinkedIn: Connect	LinkedIn: Connect
Invite additional connections, especially with people who might work for prospective employers.	Invite additional connections, especially with people who might work for prospective employers.	Invite additional connections, especially with people who might work for prospective employers.	Invite additional connections, especially with people who might work for prospective employers.
LinkedIn: Connect	LinkedIn: Connect	LinkedIn: Connect	LinkedIn: Connect
Invite additional connections, especially with people who might work for prospective employers.	Invite additional connections, especially with people who might work for prospective employers.	Invite additional connections, especially with people who might work for prospective employers.	Invite additional connections, especially with people who might work for prospective employers.
LinkedIn: Connect	LinkedIn: Connect	LinkedIn: Connect	LinkedIn: Connect
Invite additional connections, especially with people who might work for prospective employers.	Invite additional connections, especially with people who might work for prospective employers.	Invite additional connections, especially with people who might work for prospective employers.	Invite additional connections, especially with people who might work for prospective employers.
LinkedIn: Search	LinkedIn: Search	LinkedIn: Search	LinkedIn: Search
Search for job openings on LinkedIn using the Advanced Search Option.	Search for job openings on LinkedIn using the Advanced Search Option.	Search for job openings on LinkedIn using the Advanced Search Option.	Search for job openings on LinkedIn using the Advanced Search Option.
LinkedIn: Search	LinkedIn: Search	LinkedIn: Search	LinkedIn: Search
Search for job openings on LinkedIn using the Advanced Search Option.	Search for job openings on LinkedIn using the Advanced Search Option.	Search for job openings on LinkedIn using the Advanced Search Option.	Search for job openings on LinkedIn using the Advanced Search Option.
LinkedIn: Search	LinkedIn: Search	LinkedIn: Search	LinkedIn: Search
Search for job openings on LinkedIn using the Advanced Search Option.	Search for job openings on LinkedIn using the Advanced Search Option.	Search for job openings on LinkedIn using the Advanced Search Option.	Search for job openings on LinkedIn using the Advanced Search Option.
Online Research	Online Research	Online Research	Online Research
Look for job fairs and other hiring events.	Look for job fairs and other hiring events.	Look for job fairs and other hiring events.	Look for job fairs and other hiring events.
Online Research	Online Research	Online Research	Online Research
Look for job fairs and other hiring events.	Look for job fairs and other hiring events.	Look for job fairs and other hiring events.	Look for job fairs and other hiring events.

Online Research	Online Research	Online Research	Online Research
Look for job fairs and other hiring events.	Look for job fairs and other hiring events.	Look for job fairs and other hiring events.	Look for job fairs and other hiring events.
Other	Other	Other	Other
Other	Other	Other	Other
Other	Other	Other	Other

Schedule as Needed

Networking: Introductions	Networking: Thank You	Networking: Thank You	Networking: Thank You
Ask people in my network for an introduction to someone in a position to hire me.	Write a thank-you note to _____ for helping me in my job search	Write a thank-you note to _____ for helping me in my job search	Write a thank-you note to _____ for helping me in my job search
Networking: Thank you	Networking: Thank You	Networking: Thank You	Networking: Thank You
Write a thank-you note to _____ for helping me in my job search	Write a thank-you note to _____ for helping me in my job search	Write a thank-you note to _____ for helping me in my job search	Write a thank-you note to _____ for helping me in my job search
Networking: Thank you	Networking: Thank You	Networking: Thank You	Networking: Thank You
Write a thank-you note to _____ for helping me in my job search	Write a thank-you note to _____ for helping me in my job search	Write a thank-you note to _____ for helping me in my job search	Write a thank-you note to _____ for helping me in my job search
Networking: Thank you	Networking: Thank You	Networking: Thank You	Networking: Thank You
Write a thank-you note to _____ for helping me in my job search	Write a thank-you note to _____ for helping me in my job search	Write a thank-you note to _____ for helping me in my job search	Write a thank-you note to _____ for helping me in my job search
Online Research: Logistics	Online Research: Websites	Interviewing: Thank You	Interviewing: Thank You
Check out commuting logistics for desired positions.	Use LinkedIn, Glassdoor, and other relevant websites to learn about a company before any interviews.	Write a thank-you note to _____ after our interview.	Write a thank-you note to _____ after our interview.
Interviewing: Thank You	Interviewing: Thank You	Interviewing: Thank You	Interviewing: Thank You
Write a thank-you note to _____ after our interview.	Write a thank-you note to _____ after our interview.	Write a thank-you note to _____ after our interview.	Write a thank-you note to _____ after our interview.
Interviewing: Thank You	Interviewing: Thank You	Interviewing: Thank You	Interviewing: Thank You
Write a thank-you note to _____ after our interview.	Write a thank-you note to _____ after our interview.	Write a thank-you note to _____ after our interview.	Write a thank-you note to _____ after our interview.

Other	Other	Other	Other

Other	Other	Other	Other

Other	Other	Other	Other

Notes

1   Stephen R. Covey. *The 7 Habits of Highly Effective People.* Franklin Covey (Provo, UT). 1998.

2   Strict Workflow. *https://chrome.google.com/webstore/detail/strict-workflow/cgmnfnmlficgei jculkgnnkigkefkbhd?hl=en*

3   Stay Focused. *https://chrome.google.com/webstore/detail/stayfocusd/laankejkbhbdhmipfmng cngdelahlfoji?hl=en*

4   Forest. *https://www.forestapp.cc/en/*

5   Jon E. Roeckelein. *Dictionary of Theories, Laws, and Concepts in Psychology.* Greenwood Press (Westport, CT). 1998.

6   ADDitude Special Reports *(adhdreports.com). Getting Things Done with Adult ADHD.* New Hope Media (New York, NY). 2016.

7   Manuel J. Smith. When I Say No, I Feel Guilty. Bantam Books (New York). 1975.

8   Shakti Gawain. *Creative Visualization: Use the Power of Your Imagination to Create What You Want in Your Life (40th Anniversary Edition).* Nataraj Publishing, New World Library (Novato, CA). 2016.

9   National Institute of Mental Health *(https://www.nimh.nih.gov). Depression—What You Need to Know.* U.S. Government Printing Office (Bethesda, MD). 2015. NIH Publication No. 15-3561. *https://www.nimh.nih.gov/health/publications/depression-what-you-need-to-know/depression-what-you-need-to-know-pdf_151827.pdf.*

10 United States Department of Labor *(https://www.dol.gov).* American Job Centers (One-Stop Centers). *https://www.dol.gov/general/topic/training/onestop*

11 Massachusetts Executive Office of Health and Human Services, Rehabilitation Commission *(http://www.mass.gov/eohhs/gov/departments/mrc). Vocational Rehabilitation (VR) Services Overview. http://www.mass.gov/eohhs/consumer/disability-services/vocational-rehab/vr-ser vices-2.html.*

12 Massachusetts Executive Office of Health and Human Services, Rehabilitation Commission *(http://www.mass.gov/eohhs/gov/departments/mrc). Consumer Handbook for Vocational Rehabilitation (VR) Services. 2015 http://www.mass.gov/eohhs/docs/mrc/consumer-hand book-2015.pdf.*

13 CareerBuilder. *https://hiring.careerbuilder.com/company/overview*

14 Glassdoor. *https://www.glassdoor.com/about/index_input.htm*

15   Indeed. *https://www.indeed.com/about*

16   LinkUp. *http://www.linkup.com/about.php*

17   Monster. *https://www.monster.com/about/*

18   SimplyHired. *http://www.simplyhired.com/*

19   Snagajob. *http://www.snagajob.com/about/*

20   Talentzoo Advertising. *http://www.talentzoo.com/advertising-jobs/index.php*

21   College Recruiter. *https://www.collegerecruiter.com/about*

22   Talentzoo Design. *http://www.talentzoo.com/creative-jobs/index.php*

23   SchoolSpring. *https://www.schoolspring.com*

24   HigherEdJobs. *https://www.higheredjobs.com/company/about.cfm*

25   EntryLevelJobs. *https://www.entryleveljobs.net/*

26   USAJobs. *https://www.usajobs.gov/Help/About/*

27   Efinancialcareers. *http://news.efinancialcareers.com/us-en/page/about-us-2*

28   OneWire. *https://www.onewire.com/about*

29   Flexjobs. *https://www.flexjobs.com/About.aspx*

30   Good Food Jobs. *https://www.goodfoodjobs.com/about.html*

31   HealthCareJobsite. *https://www.thebalance.com/top-niche-job-sites-2061866*

32   Talentzoo Marketing. *http://www.talentzoo.com/marketing-jobs/index.php*

33   Mediabistro. *https://www.mediabistro.com/jobs/openings/*

34   CoolWorks. *https://www.coolworks.com/about/*

35   SalesJobs. *https://www.salesjobs.com/about/*

36   Internships. *http://www.internships.com/about*

37   Dice. *http://www.dhigroupinc.com/home-page/default.aspx*

38   Talentzoo technical. *http://www.talentzoo.com/geek-jobs/index.php*

39   Idealist. *http://info.idealist.org/*